Emotion Regulation Treatment of Alcohol Use Disorders

Emotion Regulation Treatment of Alcohol Use Disorders provides step-by-step, detailed procedures for assessing and treating emotion regulation difficulties in individuals diagnosed with an alcohol use disorder (AUD). The Emotion Regulation Treatment (ERT) program, consisting of 12 weekly sessions, combines an empirically supported cognitive-behavioral treatment with emotion regulation strategies to help clients manage negative emotions and cravings for alcohol. This therapist guide contains all the materials needed for the clinician to implement the program, including session outlines, detailed session content with suggestions for therapist dialogue, and client assignment for between-session skill practice. It is also designed to be used with the accompanying client workbook *Managing Negative Emotions Without Drinking*, which includes educational materials, handouts, worksheets, and between-session skill practice.

Paul R. Stasiewicz, PhD, is a licensed clinical psychologist as well as senior research scientist and director of the Addiction Treatment Services outpatient clinic at the University at Buffalo's Research Institute on Addictions. His NIH-funded research focuses on the development of novel behavioral therapies for alcohol use disorders.

Clara M. Bradizza, PhD, is a senior research scientist at the Research Institute on Addictions and a research scientist in the Department of Family Medicine at the University at Buffalo. Her research, funded by NIH, includes the development of innovative affect-based interventions for both alcohol and smoking. Dr. Bradizza is a member of the UB Institutional Review Board and is a grant reviewer at the National Institutes of Health.

Kim S. Slosman, MS, LMHC, is a clinical research project director at the Research Institute on Addictions at the University at Buffalo with more than 20 years of clinical practice and supervision experience in mental health and addiction. She also has experience delivering manualized treatments and served as a therapist on four previous clinical trials involving emotion regulation training for substance abusing clients.

Emotion Regulation Treatment of Alcohol Use Disorders

Helping Clients Manage Negative Thoughts and Feelings

Paul R. Stasiewicz
Clara M. Bradizza
Kim S. Slosman

NEW YORK AND LONDON

First published 2018
by Routledge
711 Third Avenue, New York, NY 10017

and by Routledge
2 Park Square, Milton Park, Abingdon, Oxon, OX14 4RN

Routledge is an imprint of the Taylor & Francis Group, an informa business

© 2018 Paul R. Stasiewicz, Clara M. Bradizza, Kim S. Slosman

The right of Paul R. Stasiewicz, Clara M. Bradizza, Kim S. Slosman to be identified as authors of this work has been asserted by them in accordance with sections 77 and 78 of the Copyright, Designs and Patents Act 1988.

All rights reserved. No part of this book may be reprinted or reproduced or utilised in any form or by any electronic, mechanical, or other means, now known or hereafter invented, including photocopying and recording, or in any information storage or retrieval system, without permission in writing from the publishers.

Trademark notice: Product or corporate names may be trademarks or registered trademarks, and are used only for identification and explanation without intent to infringe.

Library of Congress Cataloging-in-Publication Data
Names: Stasiewicz, Paul R., author. | Bradizza, Clara M., author. | Slosman, Kim S., author.
Title: Emotion regulation treatment of alcohol use disorders : helping clients manage negative thoughts and feelings / Paul R. Stasiewicz, Clara M. Bradizza, Kim S. Slosman.
Description: New York : Routledge, 2018. | Includes bibliographical references.
Identifiers: LCCN 2017034729 | ISBN 9781138215849 (hardcover : alk. paper) | ISBN 9781138215863 (pbk. : alk. paper) | ISBN 9781315406022 (e-book)
Subjects: | MESH: Alcohol-Related Disorders—therapy | Alcohol-Related Disorders—psychology | Cognitive Therapy—methods | Emotions | Affective Symptoms | Self-Control—psychology
Classification: LCC RC565 | NLM WM 274 | DDC 616.86/1—dc23
LC record available at https://lccn.loc.gov/2017034729

ISBN: 978-1-138-21584-9 (hbk)
ISBN: 978-1-138-21586-3 (pbk)
ISBN: 978-1-315-40602-2 (ebk)

Typeset in Sabon
by Apex CoVantage, LLC

The best way out is always through.
—Robert Frost

To our children, Adam and Hannah, who have helped us to become more patient and to value being present in the moment.
Paul R. Stasiewicz & Clara M. Bradizza

To my husband, Aaron, and my children, Mike and Kaiti, for their love, laughter, and never-failing support.
Kim S. Slosman

Contents

Acknowledgments		ix
About the Authors		x
1	Introduction and Information for Therapists	1
2	Basic Principles Underlying Emotion Regulation Treatment	14
3	Overview of General Treatment Format and Procedures	23
4	Session 1: Introduction to Emotion Regulation Treatment	40
5	Session 2: Enhancing Motivation and Mindfulness	53
6	Session 3: High-Risk Situations and Mindful Coping	63
7	Session 4: Drinking-Related Thoughts, Coping With Urges and Cravings, and Cognitive Reappraisal	77
8	Session 5: Drink Refusal Skills and Managing Emotions With Actions	92
9	Session 6: Skill and Treatment Progress Review and Preparing for Direct Experiencing of Emotion	103
10	Session 7: Coping With a Lapse or Relapse and Direct Experiencing of Emotion	111

11	Session 8: Enhancing Social Support Networks and Direct Experiencing of Emotion	128
12	Session 9: Seemingly Irrelevant Decisions and Direct Experiencing of Emotion	143
13	Session 10: Progress Review, Stimulus Control Strategies, and Direct Experiencing of Emotion	154
14	Session 11: Relapse Prevention and Lifestyle Balance	163
15	Session 12: Accomplishments and Future Directions	171

Appendix A: Common Barriers to Mindfulness Practice   177
Appendix B: Scene Development Worksheet   184
Appendix C: Individual Distress Scale   186
Appendix D: Direct Experiencing of Emotion Recording Form   187
Appendix E: Relapse Prevention Plan   188
References   189
Index   194

Acknowledgments

We would like to give a very special thanks to our colleagues Dr. Scott Coffey, Dr. Gregory Gudleski, and Dr. Suzy Bird Gulliver who shared their knowledge, expertise and friendship as we developed ERT. We are grateful to all of the clients and to the therapists who have provided us with extremely insightful feedback through various revisions and improvements to the treatment manual.

Numerous project staff including project directors, data analysts, research assistants, consultants, and colleagues have all made important contributions to this work. Our thanks go to Dr. Kenneth E. Leonard and Dr. Gerard J. Connors for contributing institutional resources that helped to support the clinical research studies on which ERT is based.

Lastly, this work would not have been possible without the generous support and funding from the National Institute on Alcohol Abuse and Alcoholism (R01 AA15064, R21 AA017115; PI: Stasiewicz) (R01 AA024628; MPI: Stasiewicz/Bradizza), National Institute on Drug Abuse (R01 DA021802; PI: Bradizza) and the Office of Research on Women's Health at the National Institutes of Health.

About the Authors

Paul R. Stasiewicz, PhD, is a senior research scientist at the Research Institute on Addictions (RIA) at the University at Buffalo. He received his PhD in clinical psychology from the University at Binghamton. He conducts clinical research on the development and evaluation of novel behavioral therapies for substance use disorders. Dr. Stasiewicz has been the director of the Alcohol Treatment Service, the outpatient treatment clinic at RIA for over 20 years. His research is funded by the National Institutes of Health and his research interests include understanding the role of craving, emotions, and learning-based processes in the development and maintenance of alcohol use disorders.

Clara M. Bradizza, PhD, is a senior research scientist at the Research Institute on Addictions at the University at Buffalo. She received her PhD in clinical psychology from the University at Binghamton. Her research has been funded by the National Institutes of Health and includes the development and testing of innovative affect-based interventions for both alcohol and smoking. In addition, much of her clinical research has focused on vulnerable populations including pregnant smokers and individuals dually diagnosed with a serious mental illness and a substance use disorder.

Kim S. Slosman, MS, LMHC, is a clinical research project director at the Research Institute on Addictions at the University at Buffalo with more than 20 years of clinical practice and supervision experience in mental health and addiction. She received her MS in Rehabilitation Counseling from the University at Buffalo. She has worked in community mental health, private practice, and clinical research settings, including providing clinical supervision for a number of studies funded by the National Institutes of Health. Her interest areas include alcohol use disorders, mindfulness, executive functioning, and Motivational Interviewing.

Chapter 1

Introduction and Information for Therapists

Rationale for Emotion Regulation Treatment

In this chapter, we describe the role of emotions in alcohol use disorder (AUD) and define several key terms including *affect regulation* and *emotion regulation*. Next, we review research that supports the development of an Emotion Regulation Treatment (ERT) approach for individuals with AUD and provide evidence of its initial efficacy. Finally, we provide an outline of ERT, its session structure, who should administer ERT, and discuss the use of the companion ERT client workbook (*Managing Negative Emotions Without Drinking: A Workbook of Effective Strategies*).

Role of Emotions in Alcohol Use Disorder

A number of theories relevant to the development and maintenance of AUD suggest that the desire to regulate one's emotional experience is an important motive underlying alcohol use. Social learning theory views alcohol use as a coping behavior that is learned as a response to unpleasant or aversive emotional states (Bandura, 1986; Maisto, Carey, & Bradizza, 1999). According to this theory, an individual's pattern of use may become problematic if alcohol is used frequently to cope with stress or other unpleasant emotions, which is most likely to happen when the individual does not possess adequate social or emotion regulation skills to manage the situation effectively. Social learning theory also emphasizes the role of cognitions to explain the role of emotional states in the maintenance of alcohol use behavior. These include self-efficacy expectations (belief that one can enact a given behavior to achieve desired outcomes) and outcome expectancies (belief about the likelihood of a behavior leading to a particular outcome). With regard to a high-risk drinking situation involving an unpleasant or negative emotion, drinking is more likely to occur if an individual has low self-efficacy for maintaining abstinence in this situation coupled with outcome expectancies that drinking will reduce or alleviate the unpleasant emotion.

Both positive and negative emotions can motivate alcohol consumption. An individual experiencing a positive emotion (e.g., joy, contentment) may drink to extend or enhance the positive emotional state. In this case, alcohol provides a source of positive reinforcement or enjoyment and this increases the likelihood that the drinking behavior will be repeated in future, similar situations. An individual experiencing a negative emotion (e.g., sadness, anxiety, irritability) may drink to reduce or get rid of the unpleasant feeling. In this case, alcohol provides a source of negative reinforcement (i.e., removal or reduction of an unpleasant or aversive stimulus) and increases the likelihood that the drinking behavior will be repeated in future, similar situations. As an individual moves along the continuum from nonproblem to problem use of alcohol, a shift occurs over time from positive reinforcement sustaining the behavior of alcohol consumption to negative reinforcement sustaining the behavior; that is, individuals who initially began drinking in order to increase enjoyment or celebrate, now are more likely to drink when feeling distressed. As part of this shift from nonproblem to problem alcohol use, when access to alcohol is prevented, a motivational withdrawal syndrome emerges that is characterized by negative emotional states (e.g., frustration, anger, irritability) (Baker, Piper, McCarthy, Majeskie, & Fiore, 2004; Koob & Volkow, 2010).

Affect Regulation and Emotion Regulation

An individual's effort to influence positive and negative affect fall under the broad heading of *affect regulation* and include the following subprocesses: (1) emotion regulation, (2) coping, and (3) distress tolerance (Gross, 2014). These three second-level regulatory subprocesses share similar functions (e.g., to reduce negative emotional responses), but can be distinguished from one another by the type of response they are meant to target. *Emotion regulation* targets characteristics of the emotional response itself (e.g., latency, intensity, duration), *coping* targets cognitive and situational antecedents of the emotional response (e.g., thoughts about the event or attempts to leave the situation), and *distress tolerance* targets behavioral reactivity (e.g., impulsive or harmful acts) to emotional responses (Linehan, 2015). ERT approaches often combine two or more of these second-level regulatory processes. While the broader term *affect regulation* may better reflect the use of these multiple, diverse strategies within a given intervention, the term *emotion regulation* has taken hold in the field as evidenced by the tremendous growth in the number of new publications over the past two decades on the topic (Gross, 2013). As a result, we have chosen the name "Emotion Regulation Treatment" for our intervention. However, given that the intervention combines *emotion regulation*, *coping*, and *distress tolerance* components, it could be more accurately termed an "affect regulation treatment."

What Is Emotion Regulation?

Gross (2014) describes the regulation of emotions as "shaping which emotions one has, when one has them, and how one experiences or expresses these emotions" (p. 6). Emotion regulation includes efforts to down-regulate negative emotions (i.e., reduce or eliminate the intensity and duration) or up-regulate positive emotions (i.e., increase intensity or duration). Further, the strategies that people use to regulate their emotions can either be adaptive or maladaptive, depending on the way they affect an individual's physical and psychological well-being (Carmody, 1989; Aldao, Nolen-Hoeksema, & Schweizer, 2010). The goals of an emotion regulation intervention would be to increase adaptive responses to the environment and reduce maladaptive responses to specific emotions. For example, substance use in response to experiencing an aversive or unpleasant emotion is a maladaptive response for a person diagnosed with AUD. In this case, treatment would aim to provide the individual with an adaptive alternative response for regulating the unpleasant emotion (e.g., Mindful Breathing, Cognitive Reappraisal, Urge Surfing). Finally, Gross' (1998, 2014) process model of emotion identifies specific points during the emotion-generative process (i.e., the point at which an emotion begins) where individuals can regulate their emotions. This model draws a distinction between antecedent-focused and response-focused strategies. Antecedent-focused strategies occur earlier in the emotion-generative process (e.g., using cognitive reappraisal before entering a stressful situation) while response-focused strategies occur later in the emotion-generative process, after the emotion is fully formed (e.g., inhibiting or suppressing the expression of an ongoing emotional response). This account acknowledges that certain emotion regulation strategies are better suited to varying intensities and developmental stage of an emotional response than others. For example, clients may derive greater benefit from applying cognitive reappraisal *before* entering a negative-affect drinking situation rather than waiting until they are in the situation and their negative emotional intensity is at or near its peak.

Theory and Research Supporting an Emotion Regulation Treatment Approach

Both theory and research support the notion that individuals who are less skilled at emotion regulation often resort to a range of unhealthy behaviors, including excessive alcohol use, in an attempt to regulate both positive and negative affect (e.g., Baker et al., 2004; Cooper, Frone, Russell, & Mudar, 1995; Cooper, Russell, Skinner, Frone, & Mudar, 1992; Koob & LeMoal, 2001; Stasiewicz & Maisto, 1993). Self-reported emotion regulation skills are lower among individuals with an AUD relative to nonclinical samples, and are comparable to other clinical samples with mental health disorders (e.g., generalized anxiety disorder, cocaine use disorders; see Stasiewicz et al., 2013). Empirical evidence indicates that poor emotion regulation skills increase risk for alcohol relapse in situations involving negative affect (Berking et al., 2011). Additionally, clinical and high-risk samples demonstrate that emotion regulation difficulties are positively associated with alcohol-related negative consequences (Dvorak, Wray, Kuvaas, & Kilwein, 2013). When coupled with deficits in emotion regulation skills, the use of alcohol to regulate emotion may be adaptive in the short term, but in the long term, drinking to regulate emotion often proves to be a maladaptive response (see Holahan, Moos, Holahan, Cronkite, & Randall, 2001; Holahan, Moos, Holahan, Cronkite, & Randall, 2003). An emotion regulation intervention proposes adding treatment components to existing cognitive-behavioral interventions for AUDs with the goal of assisting clients in becoming more comfortable with arousing emotional experiences, better able to access and utilize emotional information to engage in adaptive problem solving, and developing better skills for modulating and expressing emotions in an adaptive manner (Stasiewicz et al., 2013).

Emotion Regulation as a Mechanism Underlying Successful Treatment of Alcohol Use Disorder

Although a number of theories propose that emotion regulation is a primary motive for alcohol use (e.g., Baker et al., 2004; Conger, 1956; Cooper et al., 1995, 1992; Khantzian, 1997; Koob, 2003; Stasiewicz & Maisto, 1993), to our knowledge, there are no studies that have investigated change in emotion regulation skills as a potential mechanism of alcohol treatment effects. To date, one observational study has demonstrated that pretreatment adaptive affect regulation skills predicted less alcohol use at follow-up among patients in treatment for alcohol dependence (Berking et al., 2011). A second study has shown that abstinent alcoholics report more difficulty effectively regulating their emotions than do social drinkers (Fox, Hong, & Sinha, 2008). More encouraging, in the past decade an increasing number of studies have investigated emotion regulation processes as mediators of treatment effects for a range of mental health disorders, including borderline personality disorder (e.g., Neacsiu, Eberle, Kramer, Wiesmann, & Linehan, 2014), deliberate self-harm (e.g., Gratz, Bardeen, Levy, Dixon-Gordon, & Tull, 2015), depression and anxiety disorders (e.g., Desrosiers, Vine, Klemanski, & Nolen-Hoeksema, 2013), and social anxiety disorder (e.g., Goldin et al., 2014). While the methods employed by these studies differ (e.g., cross-sectional vs. longitudinal design, type of control group, single-group design), a common pattern of results is beginning to emerge providing broad support for the importance of adaptive emotion regulation strategies as a unifying mechanism of change underlying efficacious and effective treatments for a number of different mental health disorders.

The ERT described in this therapist guide directly targets emotion regulation as one component of a more comprehensive treatment for individuals diagnosed with an AUD. In our initial treatment development study (Stasiewicz et al., 2013), individuals who received ERT reported significant within-group decreases in negative affect, increases in cognitive reappraisal (an adaptive coping skill), and increases in observing and describing, which are both facets of mindfulness. These treatment process variables are theoretically related to ERT's two primary treatment strategies: (1) direct experiencing of emotion and (2) mindfulness. Both mindfulness and the direct experiencing of emotion (via imaginal exposure) involve similar procedures in that they both encourage contact with avoided/aversive thoughts, emotions, and sensations (Treanor, 2011). In this way, mindfulness and the direct experiencing of emotion may have a synergistic effect. For example, being mindful may enhance the direct experiencing of emotion by increasing awareness of negative affect and alcohol cues. Mindfulness may also enhance the client's ability to maintain attention on a given cue, or set of cues, during the direct experiencing of emotion. Conversely, procedures involved with direct experiencing of emotion may enhance a person's ability to observe and describe emotions, thoughts, and physical sensations. Thus, what has become clear across theoretical orientations is that exposure to avoided material, emotional arousal, and emotional acceptance and/or tolerance, are important components in the process of change in therapy (Hayes & Feldman, 2004). Future research in this area would benefit from further examination of mechanisms of change in alcohol interventions generally, and those that target emotion regulation difficulties specifically.

Identifying Emotion Regulation Difficulties in Alcohol Use Disorder

Assessment of Emotion Regulation Difficulties

Self-report continues to be the primary method by which clinicians and researchers assess difficulties with emotion regulation. The two questionnaires used most often are the Difficulties in Emotion Regulation Scale (DERS; Gratz & Roemer, 2004) and the Emotion Regulation Questionnaire (ERQ; Gross & John, 2003). The DERS is a 37-item measure that assesses self-reported emotion regulation difficulties. The DERS has six subscales that assess the following characteristics: nonacceptance of emotions, difficulties engaging in goal-directed behavior when distressed, impulse control difficulties, lack of emotional awareness, limited access to emotion regulation strategies, and lack of emotional clarity. The ERQ is a 10-item questionnaire with two subscales assessing emotion reappraisal and expressive suppression of emotion.

The Inventory of Drug Taking Situations–Alcohol version (IDTS-A; Annis, Turner, & Sklar, 1997) is administered to determine if the client reports drinking in response to negative emotions. The IDTS-A provides a profile of situations in which an individual reports drinking heavily over the past year. Heavy drinking is measured across eight subscales including Unpleasant Emotions, Physical Discomfort, Pleasant Emotions, Testing Personal Control, Urges and Temptations to Drink, Conflict with Others, Social Pressure to Drink, and Pleasant Times with Others. Participants who score above the midpoint on the Unpleasant Emotions subscale (e.g., "When I felt anxious or tense about something"; "If I was depressed about things in general") are considered to be good candidates for ERT.

Negative and Positive Emotions and Relationship to Drinking

Negative and positive emotions are the two most often-cited reasons for drinking. As noted earlier, people may drink to obtain or enhance pleasant emotion or to eliminate or reduce unpleasant emotion. Although a main focus of ERT is helping people become more accepting or tolerant of unpleasant emotions, it does not rule out the inclusion of positive or pleasant emotional drinking situations during the direct experiencing of emotion sessions (Sessions 7–10). Both theory and research provide a compelling rationale for expanding ERT to include positive affect drinking situations. First, positive and negative affect drinking situations involve appetitive responses such as craving, a highly relevant treatment target for ERT considering that craving is conceptualized as a form of affect (e.g., Baker, Morse, & Sherman, 1987; Baker et al., 2004; Tiffany, 2010). Second, despite being labeled as "positive" or "pleasant," there are several sources of negative affect in "positive affect," high-risk drinking situations that render them excellent treatment targets for ERT. For example, the experience of craving for someone trying to abstain is unpleasant and negatively valenced (e.g., Stasiewicz & Maisto, 1993; Tiffany, 1990; Sinha et al., 2009; Oliver, MacQueen, & Drobes, 2013). Often, attempts to reduce or abstain from drinking in positively valenced situations result in unpleasant feelings of loss and frustration. Attempts to abstain in these situations can also expose individuals to negative affect that may have been previously escaped or avoided by drinking (e.g., drinking at a social event to reduce social anxiety). In summary, all of these negative emotional experiences have been observed and reported by treatment-seeking individuals attempting to abstain from drinking in situations reported as "positive affect" drinking situations. Thus, although the focus of ERT is on helping individuals down-regulate negative emotions, it is uniquely suited to address the full range of drinking situations.

The Importance of Secondary Emotions

Primary emotions are innate and universal: anger, fear, sadness, happiness, disgust. Secondary emotions are emotional responses to the experience of other emotions. For example, a person may learn to feel shame in response to feeling sad or angry. In this case, sadness or anger is the primary emotion and shame is the secondary emotion. Secondary emotions are the result of a learning process. For example, a child who is belittled in the presence of others for being tearful and sad may learn to feel shame when feeling sad in the presence of others. Alternatively, a man who was punished for expressions of anger as a child may experience feelings of guilt when expressing his anger as an adult. Finally, a child who was yelled at and punished for being full of energy and laughing may become anxious when feeling excessively cheerful or happy around others. For people with an AUD, drinking may occur in response to primary emotions but it also occurs in response to secondary emotions. In our experience conducting imaginal exposure with AUD clients, secondary emotions are usually experienced as more aversive than primary emotions. Secondary, or conditioned emotional responses, are often the emotions the person is seeking to escape from or avoid by drinking. In real life, clients often report drinking prior to the emergence of secondary emotions. During the direct experiencing of emotion sessions, therapists are taught to follow the emotion as their clients' high-risk drinking situations unfold over time. Therapists are trained to identify the emergence of secondary emotions and to monitor the subsequent effect of any secondary emotion on clients' self-reported levels of craving and distress.

Development of This Treatment Program and Initial Efficacy

In a behavioral therapies development study completed by the authors, we developed and evaluated ERT (referred to as "Affect Regulation Treatment" or "ART" at that time) for alcohol dependence (Stasiewicz et al., 2013, 2014). Because ERT places greater emphasis on developing emotion regulation strategies and relatively less emphasis on specific strategies for changing drinking behavior, ERT was developed as a treatment supplement that could be used to supplement or enhance standard cognitive-behavioral therapy (CBT) for alcohol dependence. Based upon the literature linking negative affect and drinking, including the associations between deficits in emotion regulation and problematic use, ERT was designed to include cognitive and behavioral strategies addressing (1) direct experiencing of emotion (utilizing imaginal exposure), (2) mindfulness skills, and (3) several other emotion regulation skills. These emotion regulation strategies were derived from interventions that address a range of mental health disorders (e.g., panic disorder, posttraumatic stress disorder [PTSD], depression, borderline personality disorder) including substance use disorders, and differ from traditional coping skills interventions by placing greater emphasis on increasing the patient's ability to experience and regulate the subjective, physiological, and behavioral components of emotion, and less emphasis on teaching the patient how to "change" the emotion or the situational and cognitive antecedents or precursors of the emotion. Specifically, during the mindfulness and direct experiencing of emotion sessions, the therapist instructs patients to focus on the emotional response itself, and to fully experience thoughts, feelings, and sensations that are elicited by the emotional cues without attempting to escape or avoid the experiences.

In this initial treatment development study, participants ($N = 77$) received 12 weekly, individually administered, 90-minute sessions of ERT (45 min of CBT for AUD + 45 min ERT) or a Health and Lifestyles control condition (HLS; 45 min of CBT for AUD + 45 min HLS). Baseline, end-of-treatment, and 3- and 6-month posttreatment assessments were conducted. In order to justify continued development and evaluation of ERT, we felt that its impact on alcohol outcomes would have to outrival those typically found in clinical trials of CBT for AUDs. As predicted, the results demonstrated clinically significant effect sizes for increases in percent days abstinent and decreases in drinks per drinking day for ERT. Also, for nondrinking outcomes, the results revealed small to moderate effects for several treatment process variables relevant to ERT's proposed mechanisms of change (i.e., negative affect reduction, mindfulness, cognitive reappraisal).

Supporting the findings of ERT for the treatment of AUD, we conducted a treatment development study that developed and pilot tested an ERT adapted specifically to meet the challenges of smoking cessation during pregnancy (Bradizza et al., 2017). As in the alcohol study, ERT was provided as a treatment supplement to cognitive-behavioral smoking cessation treatment for nicotine dependence. Participants were randomly assigned to receive either ERT or an active control intervention similar to that provided in the alcohol study but adapted for relevance to pregnant smokers (e.g., Nutrition, Carbon Monoxide Poisoning, Managing Multiple Life Roles). Results revealed that participants who received the ERT+CBT intervention had significantly greater rates of smoking abstinence at 2-months and 4-months post-quit date as compared with the control condition participants. In addition, participants who received

ERT+CBT smoked significantly fewer cigarettes per day at 2-months post-quit date. These results demonstrate the significant impact of the ERT intervention for assisting pregnant smokers in quitting or reducing cigarette use during pregnancy. Overall, initial studies support the efficacy of ERT for reducing alcohol use among those with an AUD and, additionally, indicate that it holds promise for the treatment of other substances.

Who Should Administer the Emotion Regulation Treatment Program?

The implementation of ERT requires a moderate level of clinical skill and should be applied only by persons with the following training and professional experience: (1) graduate training in psychology/psychiatry/social work (e.g., PhD, MD, MA, MSW), (2) formal training in the delivery of CBT and exposure-based treatments (e.g., prolonged exposure, cognitive processing therapy), (3) some experience in the treatment of people with a substance use disorder, and (4) if necessary, adequate ongoing supervision. In addition to these qualifications, therapists should possess characteristics that promote emotional expression from their clients including good interpersonal skills, ability to listen to the details of negative life events, and tolerance of clients' strong emotional responses. Therapists should have an understanding of how emotional responses develop, that is, the learning of emotional responses. In addition, they should have a complementary understanding of how these emotional responses change (e.g., diminished intensity) with repeated exposure to emotional cues. An understanding of how behavioral exposure treatments work is important to effectively implementing the direct experiencing of emotion sessions. It is also helpful for the therapist to have prior experience with imaginal exposure, particularly when working with primary and secondary emotional responses that maintain substance use behavior. As with other behavioral exposure interventions, clients must "buy in" to the rationale for mindfulness and the direct and sustained experiencing of emotion. This can be more easily accomplished if the therapist has adequate knowledge of the treatment rationale and techniques and can explain them in a way that increases the client's confidence in the treatment approach. ERT should not be administered by substance abuse counselors who have not received specific training in these techniques, or are not receiving appropriate ongoing supervision and support.

Outline of Emotion Regulation Treatment Program

The ERT program consists of 12 individual, 90-minute sessions delivered weekly. A weekly session format is preferred as it provides the client time to complete assignments and practice skills introduced in the prior session. Each weekly treatment session begins with 45 minutes of CBT for alcohol dependence (adapted from Kadden et al., 1992) followed by 45 minutes of ERT-specific content. (Note: If conducting 60-minute sessions, ERT may be extended to 15 sessions.) The CBT treatment was adapted from the intervention utilized in Project MATCH, a multisite clinical trial of patient-treatment matching sponsored by the National Institute on Alcohol Abuse and Alcoholism (NIAAA). CBT is an empirically supported treatment approach for individuals diagnosed with an AUD. The main goal of CBT is to help patients achieve abstinence from alcohol by teaching them skills for managing situations that increase risk for drinking. The treatment sessions consist of skills-based content including self-monitoring, drink refusal skills, managing urges and cravings, alcohol-specific coping skills, stimulus control, relapse prevention, building a support network, and other content focused on broader strategies for achieving and maintaining abstinence.

The ERT intervention includes several emotion regulation strategies adapted from existing therapies that have specific intervention components for helping patients develop the capacity to regulate their emotions in healthy ways. Specific strategies adapted for use in ERT include behavioral analysis of interpersonal and intrapersonal drinking situations involving positive and negative affect (Sobell, Toneatto, & Sobell, 1994), behavioral coping skills that help people identify their emotions and learn distress tolerance skills (Linehan, 2015), mindfulness-based cognitive strategies (Kabat-Zinn, 1990; Segal, Williams, & Teasdale, 2002), and exposure-based strategies aimed at preventing avoidance and reducing maladaptive emotions (Foa, Hembree, & Rothbaum, 2007). The mindfulness and exposure sessions include the observing and experiencing of emotions, strategies that are designed to increase attention to the present moment and to experience the emotion without judgment or avoidance. The exposure-based sessions include imaginal presentations of individualized high-risk drinking situations involving unpleasant emotions. The personalized negative-affect drinking scenes are developed using a guided imagery worksheet that includes questions about the participant's thoughts, feelings, physical sensations, and other internal and external cues present during the affect-related drinking situation. Consistent with other imaginal exposure-based treatments (e.g., Foa et al., 2007), prior to each imaginal scene presentation, therapists instruct participants to "really feel the emotions, to accept them and remain in contact with them, without trying to suppress them or push them away."

This therapist guide is divided into chapters that provide information about how to conduct each session and suggestions for ways to present the information to the client. It is recommended that you read and become familiar with the material *before* each session, and then adapt it to suit your needs and the needs of your client. You might find it useful to practice the session content with a friend or another therapist prior to your first client. When practicing, you may find it more comfortable to use different words when describing the treatment approach, or when introducing a new treatment strategy. That's fine as long as the original meaning or intent of the treatment is retained. The *italicized* dialogue is suggested and not meant to be read verbatim to the client. It's important that you are comfortable when delivering the intervention. Like learning to ride a bike, it may be a little shaky at first, but as you work with the material in this book, you will begin to develop mastery over the material.

The ERT sessions were developed in order to accomplish the following:

1. Provide an introduction to treatment and educate the client about the role of emotions in alcohol use and relapse including the concepts of positive and negative reinforcement.
2. Provide the client with an introduction to mindfulness and other substance use coping skills and show how these skills can be used to effectively manage unpleasant emotions and urges and cravings.
3. Participate in direct experiencing of emotion via imaginal exposure to high-risk substance use situations involving unpleasant emotions.
4. Monitor weekly drinking, the connections between unpleasant emotions and drinking, and develop a plan for managing identified future high-risk drinking situations throughout treatment.

The sessions are ordered in such a way as to build upon one another. For example, mindfulness skills are taught prior to conducting imaginal exposure to high-risk drinking situations involving unpleasant emotions. These skills may enhance imaginal exposure by increasing awareness of unpleasant emotions and urges and cravings. Mindfulness skills may also enhance the client's ability to maintain attention on a given cue or set of cues during imaginal exposure.

In order for the client to fully engage with and participate in the treatment, a clear rationale should be provided and important concepts should be adequately explained. In short, the treatment approach should make sense to the client. Given the focus of this treatment on negative emotional drinking situations, a client who does not report drinking in unpleasant emotional situations, or who does not report drinking for either positive or negative emotional reasons, would not be a good candidate for ERT. Next, the alcohol-specific coping skills are not only helpful to clients for managing daily urges and cravings, but are also helpful when beginning the direct experiencing of emotions sessions (Sessions 7–10), given the propensity for these sessions to elicit emotions and cravings both inside and outside of these sessions. Teaching these skills earlier in treatment provides the client with strategies for managing these session-elicited urges and cravings.

Although therapists are expected to adhere to the general order and content of the treatment protocol, flexibly responding to clients' behavior or concerns in the moment is an important aspect of clinical practice. Treatment is viewed as a collaborative endeavor, which means that both the therapist and client will contribute to planning and directing the course of treatment. For example, while the therapist introduces the session content (e.g., Identification of Negative Emotional Drinking Situations), the client chooses the most relevant situations to discuss during the session. Further, as the therapist describes how to implement a specific treatment strategy, the client is free to modify certain elements of the strategy (e.g., when and where to practice the skill) to achieve optimal benefit. As therapists gain expertise with ERT, they will have learned what "works" from previous clients and can incorporate those ideas into the menu of options available to future clients. In this way, the therapist can tailor the treatment to a wider range of client presentations.

Session Structure

With the exception of the first session, all other sessions have five main components: (1) administer a breath alcohol test to ensure clients do not have alcohol in their system, (2) review Daily Monitoring Log and between-session skill practice since last session, (3) deliver the CBT content, (4) deliver the ERT content, and (5) assign between-session skill practice.

1. Consistent with most substance abuse treatment protocols, sessions begin with a breath alcohol test. If the client is positive for alcohol, then standard protocols for managing alcohol-positive clients are applied. If the alcohol breath test is negative, then a review of the previous week's self-monitoring record and any between-session assignments are conducted.
2. Beginning with Session 1, clients are given a Daily Monitoring Log and a between-session skill practice assignment at the end of the session. On the Daily Monitoring Log, the client is asked to record the number of drinks consumed on each day of the week, high-risk drinking situations encountered, extent of craving for alcohol, and the dominant emotion present in that situation (see copy of self-monitoring log in the client workbook). Self-monitoring can be a powerful tool to help the client identify connections between events and emotions and between emotions and alcohol use. Next, the therapist reviews between-session skill practice, reinforces the client's efforts, and troubleshoots any problems the client may have had implementing the skill.

> **Note:** The importance of reviewing both the self-monitoring record and the weekly skill practice assignment cannot be overstated. As a therapist you are giving the client these tasks because you believe strongly in their benefit to the treatment process. Checking in and reviewing these assignments lets the client know that these tasks *are* important and skill practice can help support the changes in drinking the client is seeking.

3. Following the homework review, new CBT session material is introduced followed by in-session skill practice. Next, you and client process the client's experience practicing the skill (e.g., "What was that like?" "What did you notice?"); you will reinforce the client's effort and answer any questions the client may have about the skill.
4. After delivering the CBT content, new ERT content is introduced. Procedures similar to those for teaching CBT skills (discussed earlier) will be followed.
5. After delivering both the CBT and ERT content, you and the client will negotiate a specific between-session practice assignment that includes worksheets, if any, to be completed before the next session.

Use of Client Workbook

The client workbook is written for the client and includes instructions, worksheets, and other forms to help clients successfully implement the treatment program. The therapist can either suggest to clients that they purchase a copy of the workbook or the therapist or treatment program can purchase copies of the workbook, with the cost added to the cost of treatment. We recommend that clients bring the workbook to each session. During the treatment sessions, clients can take notes or complete an in-session task directly in their workbook. They can then refer to this information when they practice the skills during the week. Clients also find it useful to refer back to previously covered material and refresh their memory for the rationale and steps for implementing a given skill.

Chapter 2

Basic Principles Underlying Emotion Regulation Treatment

Direct Experiencing of Emotions as a Therapeutic Change Process

ERT is based on two ideas that have been around for centuries. First, the tendency to avoid unpleasant emotions is a cause of suffering. Second, direct and sustained experiencing of unpleasant emotions is a way out of suffering. These two ideas can be observed in the words of Siddhartha Gautama, the writings of Sigmund Freud (1936), and the beginnings of the behavior therapy movement in the 1950s. Today, we see these ideas advanced in what has been called the "third wave" of behavior therapy with its focus on acceptance and mindfulness-based interventions. Thus, the direct experiencing of unpleasant emotions as an important principle of change has been a point of convergence of diverse therapeutic systems for centuries.

In an article published in the *American Psychologist* titled "Toward the Delineation of Therapeutic Change Principles," Marvin R. Goldfried writes:

> Therapists of varying orientations have suggested that one of the essential ingredients of change in the clinical setting involves having the patient/client engage in new, corrective experiences. The role that new experiences play in the clinical change process was initially outlined in Alexander and French's (1946) description of the "corrective emotional experience," which suggested that concurrent life experiences could change patients even without their having had insight into the origins of their problems. Alexander and French emphasized the importance of encouraging their patients to engage in previously avoided actions in order to recognize that their fears and misconceptions about such activities were groundless. They even suggested giving homework assignments to patients so that they would act differently between sessions and facilitate such corrective experiences.
> (Goldfried, 1980, p. 994)

In the case of ERT, a similar approach is employed. For example, research with a number of mental health disorders shows that treatment strategies that allow for clients to engage with negative emotions including cognitive reappraisal, acceptance, and problem solving have been associated with adaptive outcomes, including reductions in negative affect. Alternatively, emotional avoidance strategies such as rumination, suppression, and worry have been associated with maladaptive outcomes, including rebounds in negative affect and craving after encountering emotion or craving-eliciting cues (Aldao et al., 2010; Sayers & Sayette, 2013). This area of research strongly supports client engagement with and direct experiencing of negative emotion as an important step in the therapeutic change process. The direct experiencing of emotion is a guiding principle behind the development of our ERT of AUDs, and the practice of "engaging" or "staying with" (as opposed to suppressing or avoiding) the emotional experience plays a major role in many empirically supported interventions targeting emotion and emotion regulation difficulties across a range of mental health disorders (e.g., PTSD, Depression, Borderline Personality Disorder), including AUDs (e.g., Coffey et al., 2016; Stasiewicz et al., 2013).

Table 1 lists several interventions that target *emotion regulation difficulties* and includes the clinical strategy or method each intervention uses to promote the direct experiencing of emotion. While not intended to be exhaustive, the table illustrates a major point of convergence among a number of different emotion regulation interventions: namely, *the direct experiencing of negative emotion is viewed as an important step in the therapeutic change process*. Numerous investigations of this therapeutic change strategy have demonstrated that the direct experiencing of negative emotion leads to: (1) an increased ability to tolerate or accept emotional arousal, (2) reduced maladaptive emotional responses and related behaviors (e.g., conditioned emotional responses such as fear and behavioral reactivity such as substance use in response to negative emotions), (3) disconfirming of erroneous perceptions that underlie high-risk drinking situations (e.g., "If I can't drink, my irritability will be intolerable"), and (4) improved skills and increased self-efficacy for managing future high-risk situations.

As seen in Table 1, there is growing interest and evidence to suggest a common underlying therapeutic factor across a number of mental health disorders, including substance use disorders. Across these varied diagnostic categories, individuals may demonstrate increased emotional reactivity; view such reactivity as aversive; and engage in efforts to escape, avoid, or suppress emotional responding (Farchione et al., 2012). Emerging out of this perspective is the recent development of transdiagnostic interventions that target underlying common emotion regulation processes, rather than discrete, disorder-specific symptoms (see Barlow, Allen, & Choate, 2004; Berking & Whitley, 2014). Similarly, ERT embraces a core set of treatment strategies derived from empirically supported interventions

Table 1 Interventions Utilizing Direct Experiencing of Emotion That Target Affect Regulation Difficulties

Treatment	DSM-5 Diagnosis	Method for Promoting the Direct Experiencing of Emotion
Dialectical Behavior Therapy (Linehan, 1993, 2015)	Borderline Personality Disorder	Opposite Action, Mindfulness
Prolonged Exposure Therapy (Foa et al., 2007)	PTSD	*In Vivo* and Imaginal Exposure, Emotional Processing
Prolonged Exposure (modified) (Coffey et al., 2016)	PTSD w/Co-occurring Substance Use Disorder	Imaginal Exposure, Emotional Processing
Emotion Regulation Therapy (Mennin & Fresco, 2014)	Generalized Anxiety Disorder, Transdiagnostic	*In Vivo* and Imaginal Exposure
Skills Training in Affect and Interpersonal Regulation (Cloitre et al., 2002)	PTSD	*In Vivo* and Imaginal Exposure
Affect Regulation Training (Stasiewicz et al., 2013)	AUD, Nicotine Dependence	Imaginal Exposure, Emotional Processing, Mindfulness, Urge Surfing
Emotion Regulation Treatment (Bradizza et al., 2017)	Nicotine Dependence, Pregnant Smokers	Imaginal Exposure, Emotional Processing, Mindfulness, Urge Surfing
Exposure-Based Cognitive Therapy (Hayes et al., 2007)	Major Depressive Disorder	*In Vivo* and Imaginal Exposure, Emotional Processing
Mindfulness-Based Relapse Prevention (Bowen, Chawla, & Marlatt, 2011)	AUD	Mindfulness, Urge Surfing
Adaptive Coping with Emotions (Berking et al., 2011; Berking & Whitley 2014)	Major Depressive Disorder	Acceptance, Tolerance, Problem Solving
Unified Protocol for the Treatment of Emotional Disorders (Barlow et al., 2004)	Transdiagnostic (i.e., anxiety and mood disorders)	*In Vivo* and Imaginal Exposure, Behavioral Activation

that target common emotion regulation difficulties found across a range of mental health disorders.

Therapeutic Techniques That Embrace the Direct Experiencing of Emotion

Diverse therapy techniques from a number of different theoretical orientations may operate via a common therapeutic principle of change. By understanding the emotional or affective processes that account for therapeutic change, we are better able to select treatment strategies that will provide the best chance of optimizing therapeutic change. For example, the common therapeutic principles of *affective experiencing* and *corrective emotional experience* may be activated by any one or a combination of the following specific techniques: (1) exposure with response prevention, (2) role play, (3) mindfulness, (4) focusing, (5) problem solving, and (6) verbalization of emotional reactions (Tschacher, Junghan, & Pfammatter, 2014). In the treatment of alcohol use and other substance use disorders, several established therapeutic techniques that embrace the concept of direct experiencing of emotion are described as follows.

Prolonged Exposure

This treatment program is most often used in the treatment of PTSD and anxiety disorders. Prolonged exposure utilizes behavioral exposure and response prevention methods to help clients confront (rather than avoid) safe but anxiety-evoking situations (Foa et al., 2007).

Opposite Action

Derived from Dialetical Behavior Therapy (Linehan, 1993), Opposite Action is a therapeutic technique for changing or reducing unwanted emotions when the emotion does not fit the facts. Opposite Action proposes acting in a way that is opposite to the emotional urge to do or say something (Linehan, 2015, p. 362). So, speaking in public for someone who fears evaluation by others is an example of acting opposite to the urge to avoid public exposure.

Urge Surfing

This is an imagery technique for managing urges or cravings that are viewed as learned (conditioned) emotional or physiological responses to internal or external cues signaling substance use. The client imagines the urge or craving as a wave that crests and falls and washes onto shore. Clients are asked to report on various characteristics of the urge such as how the urge feels (e.g., restlessness) and where in their body they feel the urge (e.g., belly, hands). Similar to prolonged exposure and other behavioral cue exposure techniques, the client learns that the urge or craving initially increases but does subside if not acted upon (Marlatt & Gordon, 1985). In ERT, we use the term "Watch the Wave" to refer to this process.

Mindfulness

This treatment approach refers to a process of focusing on experiences in the present moment in an open, nonjudgmental, and accepting manner (Kabat-Zinn, 1990). Mindfulness stresses the momentary experience of both internal and external stimuli; however, it can be conceptualized as a form of exposure or direct experiencing in that it encourages the client to accept and make contact with (rather than suppress) unpleasant thoughts and emotions.

Kazdin (2007), writing about mechanisms of change in psychotherapy research, states, "By understanding the processes that account for therapeutic change one ought to be better able to optimize therapeutic change" (p. 4). By including several treatment techniques that share a common focus on the direct experiencing of emotion, ERT seeks to optimize therapeutic change for individuals seeking treatment for a substance use disorder.

What if Other Mental Health Disorders Are Present?

Mood and anxiety disorders frequently co-occur in individuals seeking treatment for AUD (Bradizza, Stasiewicz, & Paas, 2006), and there is evidence that the symptoms of these disorders can abate with abstinence from alcohol (Brown & Schuckit, 1988; Brown, Irwin, & Schuckit, 1991). The presence of a co-occurring disorder does not preclude treatment with ERT; indeed, many of the treatment techniques in ERT are also used to treat underlying emotion regulation difficulties in a wide range of mental health disorders (e.g., Barlow et al., 2011). However, similar to the client's substance use, therapists will want to monitor the symptoms of any co-occurring disorders and determine whether or not to recommend or administer additional treatment to address specific mental health symptoms not responsive to the ERT protocol.

Exposure to Negative Emotional Drinking Situations vs. Exposure to Traumatic Event

In prolonged exposure, a CBT for PTSD developed by Dr. Edna Foa, clients receive repeated *in vivo* and imaginal exposure to trauma-related memories and situations that elicit significant distress or anxiety. Unlike prolonged exposure, ERT does not address focal trauma nor is it intended to be a treatment for anxiety disorder symptoms. Rather, ERT targets the unpleasant or aversive emotions that precede high-risk situations for alcohol use. In this way, ERT is concerned with the functional relationship between an unpleasant thought, emotion, or physical sensation, and the person's use of alcohol.

Managing Disclosure of a Past Traumatic Event During Treatment

It is possible that during the course of treatment clients may become aware of, or disclose, a past traumatic event (e.g., sexual or physical abuse). While such disclosures can occur in any psychosocial treatment for mental health disorders, the ERT sessions that include imaginal exposure to negative emotional drinking situations may elicit memories and increased emotional responding related to a past trauma. Should this occur, the following steps will help you and the client decide on a course of action:

- Determine if the emotional response is functionally related to a high-risk drinking situation. ERT addresses unpleasant emotions that precede the client's use of alcohol. Memories, thoughts, and emotions that are related to a past trauma may or may not be directly related to the client's high-risk drinking situations involving negative emotions.
- Keep the intervention focused on the emotions that elicit the person's desire to drink. For example, extreme fear associated with a past memory of assault may not be the emotion most proximal to drinking. For example, as fear decreases, other emotions such as shame, sadness, anger, and guilt may emerge and these emotions may be most proximal to alcohol consumption. These emotions may also elicit more intense cravings for alcohol. In this example, the focus of ERT becomes the negative emotions that precede drinking rather than the fear that is directly associated with the traumatic event.
- Remember that ERT is not a treatment for trauma or PTSD. That said, there are steps that you can take that will depend on your scope of practice and your willingness—and that of client's—to directly address the traumatic event. If you are using ERT, then you are likely to be familiar with cognitive-behavioral treatments for PTSD and other disorders. If this is the case, you may feel comfortable addressing the traumatic event concurrently with ERT for AUD. There are several excellent treatment approaches available for you to consult if this is the direction that you and your client decide to pursue (e.g., Back et al., 2015; Coffey et al., 2016).
- Maintain the therapeutic focus on AUD treatment. You and the client acknowledge the trauma but resolve to maintain the focus of the

intervention on the emotions most closely associated with high-risk drinking situations. In this case, any benefits to the client's PTSD symptoms may be indirect through exposure to the negative emotions associated with drinking. If taking this course of action, then a discussion with the client about alternative treatment options for addressing the trauma is indicated.
- No matter how you and your client decide to proceed, it is important that these decisions be made collaboratively, and that you continue to monitor the impact of any traumatic event on the client's potential to benefit from ERT.

Craving and Emotion

Craving, or a strong desire or urge to use alcohol, has been added as a diagnostic symptom for AUD in the DSM-5. A common conceptualization of craving is that it is a conditioned response (CR) to alcohol cues in the environment resulting from a classical conditioning process in which one or more cues have been frequently paired with alcohol consumption. As a CR, craving has several properties that bear similarity to emotional responses. Both craving and emotional responses unfold over a relatively short period of time, have a relatively short duration (compared to more enduring moods), and give rise to behavioral response tendencies. Moreover, neuroimaging studies of craving responses show activation in brain regions also involved in emotional processing (e.g., medial prefrontal cortex, amygdala; Seo & Sinha, 2014; Phan, Wager, Taylor, & Liberzon, 2002). Similar to conditioned emotional responses, craving may be elicited by internal (e.g., thoughts about alcohol) and external (e.g., drinking contexts) cues.

Negative Emotions

One set of cues, negative emotions, have been repeatedly demonstrated to reliably elicit craving responses. In people with AUD, the craving response to negative affect is often found to be more robust than the response to positive affect (Tiffany, 2010). There is a large literature demonstrating that experimentally induced negative affect, alone or in combination with other substance-related cues, reliably elicit craving responses. For example, negative affect has been shown to enhance reactivity to substance-specific stimuli in abstinent alcoholics, opiate abuse patients, and smokers. Additionally, negative affect alone, in the absence of substance-specific cues has been demonstrated to elicit craving for alcohol and other substances (e.g., Coffey, Schumacher, Stasiewicz, Henslee, Baillie, & Landy, 2010). Thus, negative emotions are a robust set of cues that are capable of eliciting craving responses in people with AUD.

Emotion and craving responses are closely monitored during mindfulness and direct experiencing of emotion sessions.

Positive Emotions

Although negative emotional states are elevated in AUD individuals, both theory and research provide a compelling rationale for expanding ERT to include high-risk drinking situations involving positive or pleasant emotions. First, positive and negative affect drinking situations elicit appetitive responses such as craving, a highly relevant treatment target for ERT considering that craving is conceptualized as a form of affect (e.g., Baker et al., 1987, 2004; Tiffany, 2010). Second, despite being labeled as "positive" or "pleasant," there are several sources of negative affect in these "pleasant" high-risk drinking situations that render them excellent treatment targets for ERT. For example, the experience of craving for someone attempting to abstain from alcohol is unpleasant and associated with negative emotions (i.e., negatively valenced; Oliver et al., 2013; Sinha et al., 2009; Stasiewicz & Maisto, 1993; Tiffany, 1990). Attempts to reduce or abstain from drinking in positive affect situations frequently result in unpleasant feelings of loss and frustration. These feelings of frustration or loss experienced following exposure to substance-related cues is consistent with experimental data demonstrating that classic Pavlovian extinction is not a purely neutral experience. Amsel (1958) demonstrated that when a previously rewarded response is now not rewarded, the cue that previously signaled reward produced an emotional response that he called frustration. Consistent with Amsel's hypothesis, exposure and response prevention techniques such as the direct experiencing of emotion in ERT, by definition, are blocking the occurrence of a previously rewarded response (i.e., alcohol consumption). Therefore, a negative emotional response such as frustration is predicted to nonrewarded substance use cues. Third, in the absence of the drug, exposure to drug-related cues may elicit a conditioned withdrawal syndrome, a core feature of which is negative affect (Baker et al., 2004).

Negative Affect Generated by Exposure to Substance-Related Cues

As discussed in the previous paragraph, negative affect can follow exposure to substance cues and the experience of craving. The addicted individual often perceives exposure to substance-related cues, in the absence of alcohol or drug consumption, as aversive or unpleasant; O'Brien, Ehrman, and Ternes (1986) provide a compelling example. In their study of addicted opiate users, they observed an initial positive or euphoric emotional response to opiate-related cues. After several exposure trials the positive emotional response gave way to physiological withdrawal symptoms and reports of anger and frustration.

In conducting ERT, we have observed that negative emotional responses that follow unreinforced exposure to substance-related cues may be elicited by the emergence of nonsubstance-related cues (e.g., thoughts or images) that signal an aversive or unpleasant event (see Stasiewicz & Maisto, 1993, for a more detailed explanation). For example, recently abstinent individuals who are exposed to substance-related cues may experience feelings of loss. Other unpleasant or uncomfortable emotions also may emerge in this situation. In one case, a father reported drinking following an episode of anger toward his young son (i.e., yelling, threatening). These incidents typically occurred in the kitchen after his son returned home from school. After several sessions of imaginal exposure to this negative-affect drinking situation, he began to report the emergence of strong feelings of sadness and guilt about his behavior towards his young son. These emotions followed the angry outburst and emerged as he exited the kitchen by way of a staircase. On the staircase landing was a refrigerator stocked with beer. The therapist instructed the client to "pause and hold" at this point in the imaginal scene (exposure and response prevention). The client was asked to stay in that moment and to describe the context (take notice of the stairwell, the refrigerator) and any thoughts, feelings, or physical sensations that he might be experiencing. It was at this point in the temporal unfolding of the aversive event, that the client observed secondary emotions of sadness and guilt. After the imaginal scene presentation, the therapist and client processed the event and the client was astonished that feelings of sadness and guilt about his own behavior, rather than feelings of anger towards his son's behavior were motivating his drinking behavior in that moment. In this case example, the sadness and guilt were previously escaped or avoided by drinking earlier in the behavioral sequence (i.e., soon after his displays of anger, but before the emergence of guilt). Also, note that the emotions are sequentially organized in a temporal order, that is, anger first and then guilt and shame. This is a common finding in the analysis of traumatic events (e.g., Stampfl, 1991) and is a guiding principle when learning to conduct the ERT sessions involving the direct experiencing of emotion. In ERT, the therapist learns to follow the emotions taking note of those emotions that are most proximal to the client's reports of increased craving for alcohol.

Chapter 3

Overview of General Treatment Format and Procedures

Introducing the Client to Treatment

Clients come to treatment with certain expectations about the therapeutic process. Initial expectations may include receiving an appointment in a "reasonable" amount of time, for the office to be neat and clean, and for the appointment to be on time. During their appointment, they expect their therapist to listen and respond respectfully to their concerns. Additional expectations may include receiving a diagnosis or being informed of any additional tests or assessments that may be required. Finally, they expect to receive a treatment plan and information about the treatment with respect to the expected time commitment, cost, and effort. Good clinical practice will address all of these client concerns.

Clients also may have general questions about alcohol treatment, and more specifically about ERT. To help clients determine if this treatment program is a good fit for them, the following information should be provided during the first treatment session:

- ERT and standard CBT for AUDs are fully integrated in one treatment program.
- ERT is intended for individuals who report drinking in response to unpleasant emotions.
- ERT is abstinence-based, thus does not focus on drinking reduction.
- ERT is a treatment that emphasizes the acquisition of skills, thus between-session practice is important.
- ERT works best when the therapist and client work together collaboratively, therefore, honesty and respect are key aspects of working together.
- Emotions play an important role in our daily lives and in motivating problem drinking, thus time is devoted during treatment sessions to talk about emotions.
- The role of emotions in problem drinking and relapse to drinking is a focus of ERT.

More information about these topics is provided next.

Abstinence-Based Treatment

ERT is an abstinence-based treatment. Some clients, without prompting, identify abstinence as the goal of treatment. Others wish to achieve a nonproblematic level of alcohol consumption. When a client seems reluctant to embrace a goal of abstinence, it can be helpful for you to engage the client in a collaborative discussion of the topic. After acknowledging the client's autonomy to make their own decisions and eliciting any ideas the client has about the advantages of abstinence, additional thoughts to share with the client might include the following:

1. Successful abstinence is a safe choice that ensures the client won't have problems because of their drinking.
2. There can be no guarantee of a "safe" level of drinking that is certain not to cause harm.
3. For clients who might be reluctant to commit to a goal of abstinence, "sampling" a period of abstinence can provide them with opportunities that might include:

   - Exploring what it feels like to live without alcohol
   - Learning more about circumstances in which the client has come to depend on alcohol
   - Learning more about situations that trigger a desire to drink
   - Breaking existing drinking habits
   - Building confidence in the client's ability to abstain from alcohol
   - Learning and practicing abstinence-focused skills that could be useful if the client later decides to maintain abstinence

There are a number of situations in which you may want to strongly recommend that a client work toward complete abstinence. As discussed previously, this should always be done in a supportive, collaborative fashion that respects the client's autonomy. These include:

- Pregnancy
- Diagnosed medical conditions (such as liver disease) that contraindicate any drinking
- Psychological problems likely to be exacerbated by any drinking (e.g., depression)
- There exist strong external demands on the client to abstain (e.g., spouse, employment)
- Client reports the use or abuse of medications that are hazardous in combination with alcohol (e.g., benzodiazepines, opiates)
- Client has a history of severe alcohol dependence

Clients who are unwilling to consider long-term abstinence as a goal might be more responsive to intermediate options, such as a short-term trial of abstinence during treatment or a tapering off toward an ultimate goal of abstinence. In the end, clients will need to make a decision as to whether or not they are willing to commit to a period of abstinence for the duration of the treatment. If not, then a referral to another treatment program that can better address the client's needs is recommended.

Referral to a Higher Level of Care

Despite a willingness to seek out and initiate treatment, some clients are unable to benefit from weekly outpatient substance abuse treatment. They are unable to reduce their quantity of alcohol consumption, or are unable to initiate a period of abstinence. Some clients demonstrate sporadic attendance early in treatment characterized by cancellations or failing to show up for scheduled appointments. When such clients do show up for treatment, they may be intoxicated. Clients who demonstrate these patterns of behavior within the first month (up to and including Session 4) of treatment should be considered for a higher level of care, or possibly a brief stay in a detoxification program. The latter would be for those clients who demonstrate or report significant signs of withdrawal as they attempt to reduce or abstain from alcohol.

In-Session and Between-Session Skill Practice

Facilitating the Acquisition of Skills

Many behaviors are learned, maintained, and modified by positive reinforcement (i.e., the addition of a pleasant stimulus, or reward) and negative reinforcement (i.e., the removal of an unpleasant stimulus). Applying this to AUD, the underlying assumption is that these same learning processes play an important role in the development and maintenance of an AUD. ERT can help clients learn new behaviors and skills to manage situations that increase their risk for drinking. What this means for you and the client is that treatment will include the presentation of skills, followed by an in-session demonstration of the skill by you, and between-session practice exercises for the client. The general rationale for each assignment is that it promotes learning of new skills. The term *homework* is avoided because, for some clients, the word has a negative connotation. Instead, the terms *exercise, home practice activities, skill rehearsal,* or *skill practice* are used when referring to between-session practice. Individuals learn best when skills are demonstrated for them, and when they engage in practice of the skills. Therefore, a number of activities are provided to facilitate skill acquisition, including:

- Therapist demonstration of the skill
- Therapist and client role play of the interpersonal skills
- In-session guided practice of emotion regulation skills
- Client worksheets to reinforce information and skills provided in session
- Between-session skill practice

Therapist Support of Between-Session Skill Practice

You will need to provide guidance and support the client's efforts to complete between-session skill practice. Therapist behaviors that are associated with client commitment and completion of between-session activities include:

- Obtaining the client's verbal or written commitment to carry out the activity
- Defining the activity in clear and specific terms
- Engaging the client in a collaborative approach to developing the activity
- Conducting in-session practice of the activity
- Providing encouragement, particularly if the client expresses concerns about completion of between-session skill practice
- Therapist informs the client that they will be "checking in" regarding between-session practice at next treatment session
- Therapist follows up regarding completion of between-session skill practice at the beginning of the next treatment session

As discussed next, the importance of client between-session practice cannot be overstated. Similarly, checking in at the beginning of the next session conveys to the client the importance of the assignment and allows you and the client to troubleshoot any problems the client may have encountered practicing the assigned skill.

Between-Session Skill Practice: Making It Happen

Between-session practice is critical to learning new skills. A review of the literature on between-session skill practice provides guidance to therapists with the goal of maximizing the likelihood that clients will follow through with assignments. The eight steps listed next can be grouped into three higher order categories: Set-up, Negotiation, and Review.

Set-Up
1. Provide a rationale for the assignment and obtain client "buy in."
2. Increase client commitment using motivational enhancement strategies, if needed.
3. Link the assigned skill practice to the client's treatment goals.

Negotiation
4. Adapt or modify the skill to fit the client's unique needs.
5. Keep the difficulty and quantity of skill practice manageable. If necessary, break the skill down into smaller components.

Review
6. Review the prior week's skill practice at beginning of the session.
7. Provide frequent encouragement and praise.
8. Explore resistance or barriers to completing practice.

Enhance Motivation for Completing Between-Session Skill Practice

Reviewing between-session skill use and rehearsal (Steps 6–8) conveys to the client the importance of the assignments and allows you and the client to troubleshoot any problems the client may have had practicing the skills. When between-session skill practice is not completed, a brief discussion may reveal that the task was too difficult, poorly planned, or confusing to the client. Follow-up of assigned activities also provides the client with the opportunity to process or reflect upon their experience practicing the skills and whether the client felt the task was helpful.

If the client was unable to complete the between-session skill practice, explore barriers to completion. You could say, "*What prevented you from carrying out your plan as you intended?*" This should be done with care, as too much pressure may result in client resistance to exploring this topic further. Asking for the client's permission to problem solve can decrease resistance. For example, "*Would it be okay with you to take a closer look at this to see if we can find a way for you to meet your goals?*"

It is important to strike a balance between acknowledging the client's autonomy and advancing your belief that skills rehearsal is beneficial to achieving the treatment goals. Review the importance of doing the between-session skill practice with optimism and empathy. It is not uncommon for clients to have rehearsed the skills in ways that are different than what was discussed. Often, clients will modify the skill to fit their lifestyle and circumstances. Provide positive reinforcement for any attempt at between-session skill practice and reinforce adaptations that maintain the skill's intent or purpose.

Problem Solving Common Barriers to Skill Practice

In our experience, common barriers to in-session and between-session skill practice include the following client behaviors:

- Reluctance or refusal to engage in in-session or between-session practice
- Does not follow through with agreed upon between-session activity
- Refusal to continue skill practice after initial attempt
- Does not complete between-session self-monitoring forms or worksheets
- Forgets to bring between-session forms or worksheets to next session

Clients seeking treatment for an alcohol problem may vary in their motivation to change their alcohol use. Similarly, they may vary in the extent of their willingness to exert effort in the form of between-session skill practice. If the client is either reluctant to engage in skill practice or does not follow through with an assigned task, then the therapist should review either the Set-up or the Negotiation steps for maximizing client follow-through. It is most likely that the client is wavering in their understanding and commitment to skill practice, or has found that practicing the skill was unmanageable with regard to difficulty or time commitment. It is important to continue with a collaborative approach when troubleshooting between-session practice with the client. This can be illustrated in the following example:

Therapist: As I mentioned last week, we will spend the first 5 to 10 minutes of today's session checking in regarding your skill practice. How did it go this week?

Client: Umm . . . I tried to do the breathing exercise but the week just got away from me.

T: You made an attempt to try it but then couldn't get back to it because of how busy you were.

C: Well, I never did the exercise. I meant to try it, but I never found the time to actually do it.

T: When we did this exercise in session last week, you noticed how different you felt after the three breaths. You thought this could be helpful to you when things got hectic during the day. How do you feel about it today?

C: I still think this would be helpful and I do want to fit it in during my day.

T: OKAY. You still believe this could be helpful to you, but finding the time during the day has been difficult.

C: Yes. That's right.
T: I have some thoughts about how to get started. Would you be interested in hearing them?
C: Yes, because I really need to get a handle on my stress.

Thus far in the example, the therapist first reaffirms the client's commitment to skill practice. Next, the therapist asks the client if he would be willing to discuss ideas for how to fit in skill practice. The problem does not appear to be with commitment or lack of understanding of how the technique could be helpful. The client states that the technique could be helpful and is willing to engage in further discussion about how to begin using the breathing technique.

T: *Well, in my experience the majority of clients that have tried this technique have reported that it does provide relief from stress. For one thing, the breathing exercise engages the parasympathetic nervous system, which leads us to feel relaxed. This also means that the sympathetic nervous system—the one responsible for stress reactions—cannot be active at the same time. Of course, I can't say for certain that you will experience the same effects, but it sounds like you really would like to find a way to reduce your stress.*
C: *So how do I start?*

In this example, the therapist has connected the assignment to the client's goals.

T: *In my experience, most people complete their exercises in the morning—before leaving for school or work, during a break at work or school, or in the evening before bedtime. When you look at your day, which of those times would work best for you?*
C: *Definitely the evening. I'm running from the time I wake up until I crash on the couch in the evening.*
T: *It sounds like you're pretty beat by the time you hit the couch. How likely is it that you would be too tired to do one more thing?*
C: *On scale of 1 to 100, 99! All I want to do is watch an hour of TV before I go upstairs to bed. I would resent any more demands on my time.*
T: *So, doing a breathing exercise at that time might seem like another demand or a possibly a chore?*
C: *Yes, although I am here to learn healthier ways to manage my stress. You would think I'd be more eager to practice the exercise!*

T: *On the one hand, there's a tendency to view the exercise as a demand on you. On the other hand, you really want to learn some new ways to manage your stress.*
C: *I know that it really is up to me.*
T: *Yes, it is. Only you can decide what will work best for you.*
C: *You know, there is a time, right after I get into bed and before I begin reading that could work for me. I could try it then.*
T: *OKAY. You can try it out at night after you get into bed and before you pick up your book. Sounds like a good place to start.*

In this example, the client was feeling like the exercise was more of an assignment than a choice. By allowing the client to voice his frustration and difficulties with completing the assignment, the client was able to see the conflict as something that resided within himself. This freed him to make a decision that was truly his own and in his own best interest. In addition, the client was taking a manageable step by agreeing to try the deep breathing exercise once per day during a time of relatively low stress. Thus, the practice exercise was adapted to fit the client's lifestyle and tailored to fit his daily schedule. The therapist checked in with the client regarding the breathing exercise at the beginning of the following session:

T: *In our last session, you indicated that you felt you could complete the breathing practice when you got into bed for the night but before you began reading. I would like to take the first few minutes of today's session and follow-up with you about this breathing exercise. How did it go this week?*
C: *Really well. I tried it that night after our last session. I definitely felt a difference in how I felt from before the exercise compared to afterwards. It didn't take that much time and the next day I did the breathing exercise while I was having my lunch break. I felt like I got a much-needed break in my stress during the day and it didn't interfere with my work. If anything, I was more productive because my muscles weren't so tense.*
T: *So, it had the intended effect of providing some relief from your stress. That's great to hear. You even went the extra mile and tried it another time during the day. Nice. How do you feel about keeping this going?*

In this example, the therapist follows through with a review of the home practice exercise and provides reinforcement in the form of verbal praise for the follow-through.

Collaborative Therapist–Client Relationship

Delivering a manualized, skills-based intervention involves substantial direction by the therapist. However, ERT is delivered in a collaborative style with the therapist being open to and accepting of the client's input throughout treatment. As discussed earlier, examples of this collaborative style include asking permission to engage in within-session skill rehearsal, or modifying a between-session skill activity to fit the client's lifestyle. Collaboration involves continued negotiation between the therapist and client regarding treatment content and its execution.

Discussing Role of Emotions With the Client

Discuss Role of Emotions in Daily Life

Emotions are an important part of our daily lives. They enrich our experience and provide the splashes of color on an otherwise blank canvas. For example, imagine for a moment holding a newborn and not feeling joyful, or watching your favorite team lose a championship and not feeling devastated. Like most people, simply imagining these situations can trigger an emotional response! In addition to enriching our lives, emotions motivate us and guide our behavior in pursuit of goals, and they help us communicate more effectively with others. At times, our emotions can be unpleasant and even unwanted. When we experience unpleasant emotions we may try to escape or avoid them in some way. However, it is important to know that emotions, even the unpleasant ones, are an inevitable and important part of life and can, at times, even be beneficial. For example, grief over the loss of a lifelong companion can elicit comfort and social support from others whereas anger when being incorrectly charged for a service you didn't order may be appropriately channeled towards seeking repayment. Thus, unpleasant emotions can be difficult for clients to experience but do have a role in changing a client's social environment or behavior.

Role of Emotions in Problem Drinking and Relapse to Drinking

An individual's reaction to an emotion can be an unhealthy behavior. For some people, this behavior can be excessive drinking. Many people with AUD report that emotions, particularly negative emotions, lead to drinking. In fact, approximately 40% of relapse episodes have been attributable to unpleasant emotions (Lowman, Allen, Stout, & The Relapse Research Group 1996). Providing clients with education regarding the role of emotions in both drinking and relapse is an important aspect of ERT. The following provides an example of how this information can be presented to the client:

> During your evaluation, you indicated that drinking has caused problems for you and that experiencing negative emotions (e.g., anger, irritability, loneliness) sometimes leads you to drink. With

this treatment, you will learn to regulate your emotions in such a way that you attain more control over them, rather than being controlled by them. Therefore, it will be important to better understand the connection between your unpleasant emotions and drinking so that you can learn skills to better manage these emotions when they occur. While this treatment will focus more on unpleasant emotions, people with AUD also drink in response to positive emotions. However, if a positive emotion (i.e., cheerful, relaxed) triggers a desire to drink, it can be experienced as unpleasant when the goal is to abstain from alcohol. There are several reasons for this and these will be discussed in the treatment sessions. The important point to remember is that ERT will provide you with skills for managing your emotions without alcohol. The more skills available to you, the less likely you may be to drink to manage your emotions.

Direct Experiencing of Emotion Using the Therapeutic Techniques of Mindfulness and Imaginal Exposure

Psychotherapy research and practice strongly supports client engagement with and direct experiencing of negative emotion as an important step in the therapeutic change process (e.g., Barlow et al., 2004; Bowen et al., 2011; Foa et al., 2007; Linehan, 1993; Stasiewicz et al., 2013). The direct experiencing of emotion is a guiding principle behind the development of our ERT intervention for AUDs, and the practice of "engaging" or "staying with" (as opposed to suppressing or avoiding) an unpleasant emotional experience is most evident in our use of *mindfulness* and *imaginal exposure*, two therapeutic techniques that are integral to conducting ERT. To further assist clinicians who wish to use ERT in their clinical practice with AUD clients, we provide general information about how to implement mindfulness and imaginal exposure to help clients manage negative emotions related to their use of alcohol.

A solid foundation for ERT begins with providing a clear rationale for the focus on unpleasant emotions. Although clients who are best suited for ERT will have endorsed drinking in situations involving unpleasant emotions, some clients accept the rationale more easily than others. Clients who have more difficulties identifying and describing emotions, who engage in more extreme avoidance when discussing emotions, or who focus their attention externally, may be more difficult to convince. For clients who seem uncertain about the treatment rationale, you should take extra time to describe the treatment procedures clearly with the goal of helping the client understand the following points: (1) unpleasant emotions are the most common reasons for drinking among individuals with AUD; (2) urges and cravings are often experienced as unpleasant;

(3) drinking can function as an escape or avoidance behavior; (4) avoidance behaviors interfere with new learning; and (5) facing, or directly experiencing, the unpleasant thoughts, emotions, and sensations in a safe environment will result in an eventual decrease of these uncomfortable experiences. It can also be helpful for you to tell the client that greater acceptance of the rationale often requires *engaging* in one or more mindful or imaginal exposure exercises.

Suppression vs. Engagement

Talking about unpleasant emotions and urges might be considered by some people to be "off-limits" and should be avoided at all costs. Some people deny having urges and may say things like, "I don't think about drinking, I just drink." People who think this way may be engaging in *cognitive avoidance*. That is, if they admit to having an urge or an unpleasant emotion, then their sobriety may be at risk. They may feel that discussing or otherwise drawing attention to urges or emotions may trigger a relapse. Moreover, they may feel that to acknowledge an urge is to admit that treatment is not working. One example of cognitive avoidance is *suppression*. Suppression is defined as consciously pushing away unpleasant thoughts and desires. However, individuals who attempt to suppress urges and negative emotions are more likely to experience "rebound" effects (Sayers & Sayette, 2013). For example, attempts to suppress an urge may produce stronger and more frequent urges. Therefore, it's been suggested that an urge (or negative emotion) be viewed as a signal alerting the person that something is wrong and requires attention (Bien & Bien, 2002). Both mindfulness and prolonged exposure promote turning one's attention toward the unpleasant or unwanted experience rather than away from it. When used skillfully, these techniques allow the person to see that the unpleasant experience will pass. Often, the person gains a deeper understanding of what triggers these experiences and learns to "stay with" or accept the unpleasantness rather than feeling a reactive need to suppress or avoid it.

After hearing the rationale for focusing on emotions and drinking behavior, occasionally a client will say, "I don't have an emotion or craving; I just drink." In these cases it can be useful for you to talk about how well-learned behaviors happen quickly and often without awareness of any emotions or sensations that precede the behavior. In fact, research has demonstrated that people with AUD have greater difficulties identifying and labeling internal experiences such as emotions (e.g., Stasiewicz et al., 2012). However, once people with AUD begin to abstain from drinking, they learn to recognize these experiences and how they are connected to their drinking behavior.

When providing a rationale for the mindfulness exercises, clients are told that mindfulness is a skill that they will learn to assist them in developing their awareness and attention to the present moment. ERT includes several mindfulness exercises and one of the early exercises is called *Object-Centered Mindfulness* because it directs the client's attention to an *external* object and asks them to focus their attention on their *internal* sensations (e.g., touch, sight) as they manipulate the object (such as a small polished stone) in their hand. To further assist those who seem skeptical of engaging in the practice of mindfulness, you can try presenting it is an experiment. In this case, the client is asked to try the exercise while adopting a curious and nonjudgmental frame of mind. You may also indicate that many other clients have found mindfulness to be extremely useful, even those who were initially skeptical of its potential benefits. Finally, when asking a reluctant client to first try a mindfulness exercise, you can present a menu of options (e.g., Stop and Notice, Body Scan, Object-Centered Mindfulness, Mindful Observing, Mindful Breathing), and ask the client to choose among them. Instead of asking "Will you do this exercise?" the question becomes, "Which exercise do you want to do?"

In ERT, you begin by teaching clients brief awareness activities like Stop and Notice and Body Scan. When teaching these skills, you are asking clients to direct their attention to their experience in the present moment. In this way, the mindfulness skill practice serves as preparation for directing clients' attention to the unpleasant emotions they will experience during the *imaginal exposure* sessions. The mindfulness practice compliments the direct experiencing of emotions because it helps clients develop their awareness of the different facets of an emotional event and helps sustain their attention to these experiences as they unfold over time. Unpleasant or distressing emotions and memories can challenge a client's attention during any therapy. Through in-session and between-session practice of skills, clients enhance their ability to attend to, and tolerate, the discomfort of different emotions, cravings, and physical sensations. The goal is to help clients recognize the impermanence of these unpleasant experiences and to weaken the connection between these experiences and alcohol use.

Conducting the Direct Experiencing of Emotion via Imaginal Exposure

Presenting the Rationale

The rationale for direct experiencing of emotion is explained in detail in the first treatment session. Briefly, clients are told that drinking to escape or avoid unpleasant emotions, thoughts, and physical sensations is an important factor that maintains their problem use of alcohol. Because avoidance of negative emotions can maintain alcohol use, ERT encourages clients to face these experiences as a way to manage them. Finally, the client is told that direct experiencing of negative emotional drinking situations via *imaginal exposure* is an effective strategy for reducing the intensity of the unpleasant emotions and cravings and can increase confidence for managing future high-risk situations without drinking. The rationale is repeated in each subsequent exposure session to help maintain the client's engagement with the direct experiencing of emotion and to reinforce the effectiveness of *imaginal exposure* as a method for breaking the connection between unpleasant emotions and alcohol use.

Conducting Imaginal Exposure to Negative-Affect Drinking Situations

The goal of direct experiencing of emotion is to weaken or break the *emotion–craving–drinking* connection. To accomplish this goal, two conditions must be met. First, exposure should activate both emotion and craving responses that are the targets of ERT. That is, exposure should be conducted in a way that promotes engagement with the complexities of distressing emotions and cravings within the safe context of the therapist's office. Second, *imaginal exposure* should include corrective information that can then be incorporated into the complex emotion–craving–drinking experience. For example, a AUD client who repeatedly recounts a negative emotional drinking situation in successive sessions (Sessions 7–10) and experiences a decrease in distress and a decline in emotion-elicited craving learns that thinking and talking about negative emotional drinking situations does not invariably lead to drinking or loss of control and that both the unpleasant emotions and cravings associated with thoughts about the high-risk situation will eventually subside.

During *imaginal exposure*, the client is instructed to visualize and describe the context and their emotions and cravings associated with an individualized high-risk drinking situation. To facilitate engagement with their emotions and cravings, clients are encouraged to keep their eyes closed and to use the present tense when describing the events as they unfold. You will prompt for details periodically (i.e., emotions, thoughts, physical sensations, context), but not so frequently as to disrupt the client's emotional engagement with the imagery scene. Also, you will monitor the client's level of distress and craving throughout exposure scene.

As the client engages with the imagery scene, you will use the client's ratings of distress and craving to direct the client's movement in the scene to those elements (e.g., thoughts, actions, sensations) that elicit strong emotion and craving responses. When the direct experiencing of emotion is effective, the client is engaged with the various components of the emotional response (i.e., thoughts, feelings, sensations), but remains grounded in the present. Thus, the client recounts the emotion-related drinking situation knowing that he is safe and that the emotions and cravings, although challenging, will eventually decrease without needing to turn to alcohol or another unhealthy behavior to manage them. Your task during imaginal exposure is to keep the client's attention focused on those aspects of the situation that elicit emotion and craving, and to prevent the client from engaging in cognitive and behavioral escape or avoidance responses. If the client engages in avoidance behaviors, this will disrupt processing of both emotion and craving responses as these avoidance behaviors prevent the client from learning that the emotion and craving will eventually subside.

Emotional Under-Engagement in Imaginal Scenes

There are times when the client is not effectively engaged with the emotional or craving content of the imaginal scene. In prolonged exposure (Foa et al., 2007), this is referred to as *under-engagement*. Reasons for under-engagement include:

- Inadequate situation selection
- Misunderstanding of exposure rationale
- Use of distancing strategies (e.g., use of past tense to describe imaginal scene)
- Use of cognitive and behavioral avoidance strategies (e.g., mental compulsions, suppression, changing contexts within the scene as emotion and craving reaches its peak)
- Imagining drinking or making the decision to drink while engaged in the exposure
- Beginning a scene after the client has already consumed alcohol in the imaginal scene (if this happens, restart the scene at a point before any alcohol is consumed)

Often, brief questions that probe for details about the context, physical sensations, emotions, and thoughts can increase the client's engagement in the imagery scene. Sample questions can include:

- *Turn to your left. What do you see?*
- *Look at her face. What do you see?*
- *What are you thinking?*
- *Where in your body do you feel that?*
- *Where is the alcohol located?*
- *What does the glass/bottle feel like in your hand?*

Client responses to these and other brief probing questions may introduce additional cues that the client has not yet volunteered and that can intensify emotion and craving responses. To keep the client engaged in the imaginal exposure, it is helpful for the therapist to ask these questions in the present tense and to allow sufficient time for the client to respond and integrate the information into the scene. Asking too many questions in a row can be disruptive to the client's emotional engagement in the scene.

If under-engagement continues to be problematic, check for the client's understanding of the rationale for exposure and whether the situation is appropriate. Problems with scene selection may involve choosing a past event with little or no chance of recurring, a situation in which the client reports no longer drinking, or the client inaccurately specifies the timing of the relationship between their experience of distress and their experience of craving. For example, the client may report experiencing stress while at work, but does not report craving until driving home at the end of the work day. In this case, the client knows that he will not or cannot drink at work and therefore does not crave a drink while still at work.

Finally, client under-engagement may be the result of certain mental compulsions that remain unobservable to the therapist. Mental compulsions may involve words, images, phrases, or prayers that clients repeat to themselves to neutralize uncomfortable emotions and cravings or prevent a feared outcome such as loss of control or a return to drinking. Similar to behavioral avoidance, mental compulsions (i.e., cognitive avoidance) are problematic because they are negatively reinforced by preventing direct exposure to more fearful or distressing images and thoughts. The mental compulsions are then maintained, which leaves the client vulnerable to relapse because the emotions and cravings associated with the more distressing thoughts and images are maintained. It's important to distinguish between an obsession and a mental compulsion. Whereas an obsession is an intrusive thought that *increases* distress, a mental compulsion is a cognitive act that *decreases* distress. A common mental compulsion that can disrupt the process of exposure with AUD clients is repeating the phrase "drinking is not an option." When a mental compulsion is identified as a reason for under-engagement, the therapist will educate the client about the function of such mental statements and instruct the client to refrain from this type of cognitive avoidance during the imaginal exposure scene. That is, clients are told that they can allow thoughts that provoke emotions and cravings (e.g., "A drink would be really good right now."), but that they need to avoid thoughts that aim to decrease these responses (e.g., "Drinking is not an option").

Emotional Over-Engagement in Imaginal Scenes

Another potential area of concern when conducting the direct experiencing of emotion is *over-engagement*. When considered in the context of ERT with AUD clients, this nearly always refers to clients who, during imaginal exposure, have difficulty maintaining a sense of safety and control as it relates to their sobriety in the present moment. In the client's mind, recounting a negative emotional drinking situation and re-experiencing strong cravings is a threat to their sobriety. In its most extreme form, the client's level of distress may be very high, but the distress is related to the emergence of a craving response. At this point, the client may engage in one or more attempts to escape or avoid the distress including removing himself from the imaginal scene. Here again, certain procedural modifications may help to decrease over-engagement during imaginal exposure. As in under-engagement, first restate the rationale for the direct experiencing of emotion. Explain to the client that thoughts and images are not inherently harmful, and that "watching" them as they rise and fall away can be very helpful to their long-term sobriety. It's also important in these moments for the therapist to convey empathy and compassion for the client's struggle and to provide encouragement for facing a very challenging situation. Finally, if the client seems unable to move beyond this point in the exposure, then the therapist may direct the client to use a coping skill to foster a sense of self-control and confidence in being able to manage unpleasant emotions, sensations, and cravings. For example, directing the client to take in three deep, mindful breaths can help move the client past the most difficult moment in the scene. However, in a situation in which the client is over-engaged, it is often more helpful if the therapist asks the client if there are other things that could be done in the moment to facilitate the client feeling safe and supported.

Conclusion

This program creatively combines empirically supported clinical strategies used in the treatment of both emotion regulation difficulties and AUDs. Thus, ERT provides another tool for treatment providers that can positively impact the lives of AUD individuals, which are often severely disrupted by alcohol use. The information presented in this chapter provides a broad overview of ERT and prepares you to discuss the main components of the intervention (i.e., abstinence-based treatment, skills-based treatment, collaborative relationship, focus on relationship between emotion and drinking, direct experiencing of emotion) with your clients. However, we recognize that the very nature of an addictive behavior may hinder some clients' ability to engage in, and benefit from, ERT. It is not uncommon for people with AUD to attend treatment sessions inconsistently or to drop out of treatment prematurely. Many struggle with identifying and managing their emotions, engage in escape or avoidance behaviors, and often do not complete the between-session skill practice. For these clients, it is helpful if the therapist can demonstrate flexibility in the use of both the CBT and ERT clinical content. The emphasis on a collaborative therapeutic relationship should help you formulate a clear path forward that is shared by both you and your client.

Chapter 4

Session 1
Introduction to Emotion Regulation Treatment

Materials

Managing Negative Emotions Without Drinking workbook, Chapter 3
Therapist Body Scan Script, located in this chapter

Session Overview

In this session you will establish rapport and begin to engage the client in the treatment process. You will review the structure and nature of the treatment program including the goal of abstinence and importance of active skill practice within and between sessions. Education will be provided to the client regarding the ways in which alcohol and emotions interact and you will begin to explore how their own drinking may be related to their emotional experiences. The purpose of emotions and the importance of engaging with their emotions rather than avoiding or escaping them will be explained. By exploring the nature of emotions, the client will gain an increased understanding of alternative approaches for regulating and coping with emotions. Mindfulness will be introduced, practiced in session, and assigned for between-session skill practice.

Session Outline

- Session introduction
- General treatment overview
- Emotions and alcohol
- Managing emotions
- What are emotions and how do they protect us?
- In-session skill practice: Body Scan
- Between-session skill practice

Session Introduction

Conduct Breathalyzer Test

You should inform the client that each session will begin with a breathalyzer test to ensure that the client is alcohol free. If the client is not familiar with a breathalyzer, you should describe the procedure in advance, in order to increase the client's comfort level. Once the test is completed, you can invite the client to turn the device around and look at the reading.

Therapist Background and Qualifications

At this point, you should provide the client with a brief description of your educational background, credentials, and professional experience. This provides the client with important information about your skill and experience, and can positively impact the client's confidence in your abilities.

Client Rapport and Engagement

At this point, transition to a discussion that supports the development of the therapeutic relationship, and engage the client in the treatment process. This can include a discussion of the collaborative nature of the treatment. In addition, you can use this as an opportunity to get to know the client, their reasons for entering treatment, and their drinking patterns and motivations. It is also useful to learn more about the client's previous quit attempts and their expectations regarding what treatment will be like. Sample questions include the following:

- *Tell me a little about what brought you here.*
- *How do you spend your free time?*
- *What happened recently that helped you to make the decision to enter treatment now?*
- *Have you ever been to counseling or treatment for an alcohol or drug use problem?*
- *What were your experiences like?* (If the client dropped out of treatment, explore specific reasons.)
- *Have you ever tried to quit on your own?*
- *What was that like?*
- *In what kinds of situations or circumstances do you drink? Can you give me a specific example?*
- *When you think about alcohol treatment, what do you think about? That is, what is your idea of what treatment should be like?*
- *What are your goals for treatment? What do you hope to get from treatment?*

The therapist should reflect and summarize the information the client has shared thus far including what brought them here, where they are in terms of commitment and ambivalence about stopping drinking, what they might want from treatment, and any other information that seems significant to the client.

General Treatment Overview

Provide the client with a description of treatment including the skill-based nature of the intervention, and that it consists of 12 individual weekly sessions that are approximately 90 minutes in duration. Each session begins with a review of the client's between-session skill practice, and includes fine-tuning skills and problem-solving barriers to implementing skills. New information, skills, and strategies directed towards achieving and maintaining abstinence, and managing emotions will be introduced, along with plans for using these skills in the upcoming week.

> *The number and duration of our sessions gives us the time we need to work on the skills to help you make changes to your drinking. It also will provide time for you to "try out" the skills by practicing them first during our sessions. This way, you will be more comfortable using them in your daily life.*
>
> *At the beginning of each session, we will talk about how things have been going for you, whether the new skills have been helping, and if they need any fine-tuning to work more effectively. We'll also review times when you wanted to drink or did drink, learn more about these situations, and make a note of any alcohol that you might have had. We will then talk about new skills or strategies that you can use to help you abstain from drinking, cope with situations that might be related to drinking, and adapt the skills to your specific drinking situations. We'll also keep building your understanding and skill set for managing the emotions that could be getting in the way of the sobriety you want for yourself. These are skills that everyone could benefit from, skills that can be used to manage life's challenging moments.*

> **TIP** People vary in their ability to identify and describe their emotions. Early in treatment, it may be preferable for you to use words or terms that your client uses when referring to emotions (e.g., stressed, upset, wiped out, keyed-up). As treatment progresses, a shared emotional vocabulary will develop between you and your client.

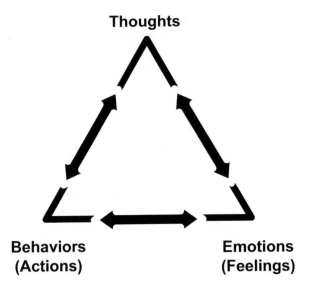

Figure 1 Cognitive Behavioral Model

Introducing the basic CBT model (Figure 1) of the relationship between thoughts, feelings, and behavior can enhance the client's understanding and motivation to use the strategies described in treatment. This brief description is not intended to result in a thorough understanding of the intricacies of CBT, but rather to give the client a basic understanding of "how things work." It should provide a working model from which to operate throughout the course of treatment.

As each session focuses on various aspects of CBT, the client may be oriented to the model as a reminder of how that session's strategies work to accomplish the change that is desired by the client.

Emotions and Alcohol

This section provides information regarding how emotions motivate drinking behavior, followed by a discussion of the specific strategies that will be taught during treatment to help the client manage difficult emotions without drinking:

> Drinking alcohol to manage or enhance emotions is common. Sometimes people drink when they feel good, to make the good times even better. People also drink when they experience unpleasant emotions. For example, when they are bored or have to complete an unpleasant chore, they may grab a favorite alcoholic drink to help them get started and make it more pleasant. At the end of a stressful week, a

person may decide to unwind with a few drinks. At times, people may have quite a few drinks in response to an emotionally painful event such as a relationship break-up or the loss of a job. Depending on the circumstances, drinking in this way may not lead to a problem, particularly if the amount of alcohol consumed is relatively low, or this doesn't happen very often.

Often, people reach for alcohol in order to regulate their emotional experiences because alcohol can change how they feel. Sometimes people drink "ahead of time," before a stressful situation, to avoid uncomfortable feelings. If alcohol is regularly used in this way, this can become a habit. In fact, people can become so efficient at using alcohol to manage their emotions before a stressful or unpleasant event that they are not even aware of the connection between alcohol and their emotions. A person may also reach for alcohol to manage racing thoughts or memories that fuel emotional distress or to prevent themselves from saying or doing something they will regret later. Does this make sense? Have you ever noticed people doing this?

As it turns out, the vast majority of people drink at times or in situations that involve either positive or negative emotions. For people with AUD, we know that up to 40% of relapses to alcohol are in situations that involve unpleasant emotions and this percentage goes up to 75% if we include situations that involve conflict or disagreements with other people. Is it possible that something like this is having an impact on your use of alcohol? Would you be willing to explore how emotions and drinking may be connected for you?

Explore client's use of alcohol in unpleasant emotional situations with a focus on more frequently occurring situations.

Although some people can use alcohol in response to emotions without experiencing negative consequences, for other people, problems can develop over time. A person may find they are turning to alcohol more often during the week or that the amount of alcohol they consume starts to increase. Other life areas may also begin to be negatively affected such as strained relationships, poor health, or legal consequences, such as a DWI. Sometimes the impact of alcohol use may have more subtle effects. For example, a person's thinking isn't as clear or sharp as it used to be. It is also possible that a person stops pursuing activities that they used to enjoy. The use of alcohol may begin to get in the way of being the kind of worker, parent, or partner they want to be.

When a person decides to make a change in their drinking, the habit of using alcohol to manage emotions can present some specific challenges. The use of alcohol to reduce emotional discomfort

Session 1: Introduction to ERT

is reinforcing; the more often someone uses alcohol to reduce emotional discomfort, the stronger the desire to drink can become. Like a tropical storm that becomes a hurricane, this unhealthy cycle continues to strengthen with each repetition, becoming a habit that can be very difficult to stop. The use of skills, such as those taught in this program, can help to interrupt this process and assist people in changing their drinking. Just as important, these skills can help maintain the changes they have made in their drinking. In this program, you will learn a variety of ways to manage or regulate emotions without drinking alcohol. Let's take a moment and review those now.

Managing Emotions

Mindfulness

The first strategy for managing emotions that we will discuss is mindfulness. Mindfulness involves being aware in the present moment in a purposeful way. When some people hear mindfulness, they think only about meditation. Although meditation is one of the ways that people can be mindful, there are many different ways and we will learn several of them over the course of treatment. What comes to mind when you hear the word mindfulness?

Taking Action

A second strategy involves taking action. One of the most effective ways to change a pattern of behavior is to begin by taking concrete steps towards making changes. When we take steps to do something different, we make room for the rewards of new, pleasurable experiences in our daily life. Even small steps can set you on a path to making effective changes. A few examples of this include taking the dog for a walk and enjoying the outdoors, making plans to have dinner with a friend who supports your abstinence, renting a movie or catching up on an episode of a favorite TV show.

Direct Experiencing of Emotion

A third strategy involves directly experiencing unpleasant emotions using a technique called imaginal exposure. In Sessions 7–10, you will be asked to recount and experience a high-risk negative emotional drinking situation. Repeated and direct experiencing of these unpleasant emotional sessions can be effective in reducing the intensity of our negative emotional responses and related urges, cravings, and physical sensations. Often, people become more aware of the emotions and sensations that provide the motivation for drinking. As you develop greater awareness of the connection between uncomfortable experiences and your use of alcohol, you can respond with greater flexibility in managing these emotions when they occur.

Cognitive Reappraisal

A fourth strategy for managing your emotions is called Cognitive Reappraisal. This strategy targets your thoughts because the way you think about or interpret a situation can influence how you feel. If you focus exclusively on the negative aspects of a situation, then you will more likely experience an unpleasant emotion. However, if you can challenge yourself to come up with one or two alternative ways of thinking about the same event, then you may be able to decrease your level of emotional distress to manageable levels.

Summary

So far, we have talked about the role emotions play in motivating drinking and some of the strategies that you will learn to help manage unpleasant emotional drinking situations. With this treatment, you can learn to regulate your emotions such that you can gain more control over them, rather than being controlled by them. Therefore, it will be important to better understand the connection between emotions and drinking so that you can learn skills to better manage these emotions when they occur.

TIP If the client does not see a connection between alcohol and emotions, you may approach the discussion using the idea of drinking as a habit that has become automatic:

When driving, we often don't think a lot about our actions; we usually just drive on "automatic pilot." But what if someone reversed the gas and brake pedals? Now we would need to give more thought to driving—we would have to pay closer attention. If we apply this analogy to drinking, often people can drink on "automatic pilot"; they don't give much thought to what motivates them to drink. When people try to change their drinking, it can take a bit more effort or thought, at least at the beginning, to do something different. They may need to pay attention to the cues that trigger urges or cravings to drink. A better understanding of when and why they drink can help them to make these changes.

What Are Emotions and How Do They Protect Us?

To manage emotions effectively, it is helpful to know a few things about how they work. We know they range from very pleasant to very unpleasant and that all emotions are important. They help us live life to the fullest and are necessary for our very survival. Pleasant emotions play an important role in our well-being. If we accomplish a difficult task, we tend to feel proud of ourselves. These feelings will likely motivate us to try that task again or to try similarly difficult tasks. Pleasant emotions can help us build closer, more satisfying relationships with others.

Sometimes we think of pleasant emotions as "positive" and unpleasant emotions as "negative"; however, the unpleasant emotions aren't really negative or "bad" because they serve a very important purpose, in the same way that pleasant emotions do. It makes sense that we don't necessarily like or want to experience the discomfort of unpleasant emotions but it is the discomfort that makes them so effective. Their job is to get our attention and urge us to do something to make the discomfort go away. For example, if we see a vicious dog, we'd probably feel frightened and prepare to stand and fight or run away. Like a fire alarm going off, these distressing emotions grab our attention, warn us to protect ourselves, and urge us into action to secure our safety. It's because the emotion is uncomfortable that we take action.

TIP If a client expresses confusion about possible actions in a given situation, the therapist can respond as follows:

> *There may be times in our lives when we are unable to take immediate action to solve a problem. For example, a failing relationship or financial pressures are not easily solved and may persist for weeks or months. With these examples, the chronic emotional distress may need to be addressed, even if the problem itself cannot be remedied quickly. Coping skills can help us manage the day-to-day distress, decreasing it to a manageable level and creating a better state of mind in which to think more clearly about solutions to the problem.*

Alcohol interferes with the healthy functions of emotions, stopping them from serving their purpose. It can take away the immediate discomfort of unpleasant emotions by way of its temporary numbing and relaxing effects. However, without the unpleasant emotion to motivate a person to take positive action, existing problems may stay the same or get worse. Feeling that urge to take an action is just one aspect of emotions. Other aspects include physical sensations, thoughts, and behaviors. So, let's say you are experiencing an emotion such as anger because you have a disagreement with a friend or family member. You may feel the urge to storm out or to pick something up and throw it. Your actions may include yelling or slamming doors. You might be thinking "He never listens to me!" or "I can't believe this happened again!" Some physical sensations you may notice are muscle tension, your heart racing, and tightening in your jaw. Emotions vary in their strength or intensity and in their duration. Often, they come and go, like waves. Although it may not seem like it at the time, an important feature of our emotions is that they are temporary, so you can ride them out.

Increasing Emotional Awareness

In the examples I just mentioned, the exact emotion a person is feeling may seem obvious, but in everyday life it can be more difficult to figure out. Often people aren't aware of what they're feeling or what caused them to feel a certain way. Just think how common it is for people to be going about their day with their shoulders tense and tight, and not even realizing it until their shoulders start to ache or they develop a headache.

Body Scan

So, one of the first steps to managing emotions without alcohol is to become more aware of them. It is difficult to manage an emotion if you don't know it's there or if an emotion becomes too strong, making it more difficult to manage. Since physical sensations are one of the components of an emotion, it is a good place to start. I'd like to start by introducing you to a technique for identifying and noticing physical sensations. Most people find it easier if they close their eyes; this way you can "tune in" without your brain being distracted by the things you see. I'll guide you through it, so you can get a better idea of the process.

Body Scan Script

> **TIP** Pauses are included in the script to allow the client to focus on their sensations. Please note there are shorter and longer pauses:
>
> . . = 1–2 second pause
> . . . = 3 second pause

> The periods may be counted silently as you read the script (e.g., *Notice any sensations you may have in your elbows . . . forearms . . . hands . . .* would be read as *Notice any sensations you may have in your elbows* (one, two) *forearms* (one, two) *hands* (one, two), etc.)

Allow your eyes to gently close (or leave them slightly open if that is more comfortable). Place your feet on the floor, and let your body settle, relaxing into the chair, feeling the weight of your body on the chair . . .

Take a few slow deep breaths . . . (You can model breaths for the client to follow along, without pausing or holding the breath between the inhale and exhale. Pause 10–15 seconds.)

This Body Scan is about "just noticing" whatever you may be feeling in your body. The goal is not to change anything about what you are feeling, but rather to direct your attention to various parts of the body, becoming aware of any sensations you may be experiencing in the present moment.

Starting with your head, notice any physical sensations you are having in your scalp . . . ears . . . eyes . . . and mouth . . .

Shifting your attention down now to your jaw . . . throat . . . neck . . . and noticing whatever is there . . . or maybe feeling nothing in particular . . .

Bringing your awareness to your shoulders, and scanning them for any kind of sensations . . . warmth, coolness, tightness . . .

Shifting your attention to your back . . . noting any sensations you are having . . . the pressure of your back against the chair . . . your clothing against your skin.

Some sensations might be pleasant . . . or neutral . . . or unpleasant. Try not label them as good or bad, just notice them, and let them be.

Now tuning in to your stomach . . . your chest . . . aware of how sensations move with the breath, as it comes and goes, following the sensations of your breath, not trying to breathe any certain way . . .

Feeling now your upper arms . . . lower arms . . . and hands . . . becoming aware of any sensations, tingling, tightness, pressure where your arms are resting against something . . .

If you become aware that your mind has drifted to something else . . . this is what minds do . . . just acknowledge where it went, then gently guide your attention back to the body.

Now shifting your attention to your hips . . . thighs . . . knees . . . and noticing whatever is there . . .

Bringing awareness to your lower legs, calves . . . shins . . . feet . . . and toes.

> *Feeling your feet inside your shoes . . . noticing the bottom of your foot against the sole of the shoe . . . feeling the support of the floor beneath your shoes . . .* (5 seconds)
> *Moving back up now, and building an awareness of your body as a whole . . . the legs and hips . . . stomach and chest . . . shoulders, neck, and head.*
> *Noticing your body as a whole . . . its sitting position . . . how that feels. . . .* (5 seconds)
> *Shifting your attention now to the sounds around you . . .* (5 seconds) *. . . noticing any differences between sounds . . .* (5 seconds)
> *Gently allowing your eyes to open . . .*

Dedicated Mindfulness

This treatment program refers to formal mindfulness practice as "Dedicated Mindfulness" in order to highlight the importance of setting aside time that will be "dedicated" to this practice and to reduce potential hesitation to engage in something that might be misconstrued due to alternate meanings of the word *formal* such as "reserved, prim and proper, stiff, strict" and so on.

The Dedicated Mindfulness practice for this session will be the Body Scan.

Stop and Notice

The "Stop and Notice" skill is necessary for building awareness and is a precursor to informal mindfulness practice, which will begin at Session 3.

> *"Stop and Notice" is a skill that is introduced today and will continue to be called on in future sessions as well. It means just what it says: From time to time throughout the day, take a moment to slow things down, and just "Stop and Notice" what you see around you, what you hear and feel, your thoughts, emotions, or desire to drink, and what you are doing in the present moment.*
> *This practice can sometimes be calming, while at the same time helping you become more aware of what may be contributing to the problem drinking. The more information you have about this, the better able we will be to develop a plan that will help you reach your goals.*

Daily Monitoring Log

Review the Daily Monitoring Log and demonstrate its use by using one of the client's own examples. Note that some of the columns may be difficult for the clients to complete. Briefly mention that the desire to drink can come in the form of thoughts, cravings, and urges, and can range from very mild, like a passing thought (1) to very intense (100).

> *This daily self-monitoring log is a very important tool that we will use at every session. It helps us identify times when it may be more difficult for you not to drink. It will also help you become more aware of what may be putting you at a higher risk for drinking. Here is where you can make a note of what you observe when you "Stop and Notice." This log will be most effective if you complete it daily. We will review your monitoring log together at the start of each session.*
>
> *Remember that you don't have to write a lot. It's okay if you're not sure what to write in some of the columns; that's why we set aside time at the beginning of each session to go over it. As time goes on, you'll see how this information can help you achieve your goals. With each session, it will become easier to know what to write.*

What Your Client Hopes to Gain From Treatment

> *Before our next session, please give thought to what you would like to gain from coming to treatment and complete the section at the end of the Chapter 3 in the workbook titled, "What I Hope to Gain From Treatment." We will discuss at the next session.*

Between-Session Skill Practice

> **TIP** The term *homework* is avoided because, for some clients, the word has developed a negative connotation. Instead, the terms *exercise, assignment, home practice activities, skill rehearsal,* or *skill practice* are used when referring to between-session activities.
>
> Tell the client that you will "check in" at the beginning of the next session. This conveys to the client the importance of the assignment and allows you and the client to troubleshoot any problems they may have practicing the assigned skills.
>
> Work collaboratively with the client to develop a plan for between-session skills rehearsal. The plan will involve the specific skills to be practiced and the frequency and duration of each practice exercise. On the next page, you will see recommendations for skill practice. These are guidelines to use when developing the between-session skills practice plan with your client.

- Practice the Body Scan exercise for 5 minutes twice daily.
- Practice "Stop and Notice" four or more times daily.
- Review the Physical Sensations That Often Accompany Emotions handout and the Emotions List at the end of Chapter 3 in the workbook.
- Complete the Daily Monitoring Log each day.

Making It Happen

- Build it into daily life.
- Think about when and where to rehearse the skills.
- Cue yourself to remember to practice the skills.

Chapter 5

Session 2
Enhancing Motivation and Mindfulness

Materials

Managing Negative Emotions Without Drinking workbook, Chapter 4
Therapist Brief Body Scan Script, located in this chapter
Therapist Object-Centered Mindfulness Script, located in this chapter
Items for Object-Centered Mindfulness exercise

Session Overview

In this session, you will conduct a decisional balance exercise of the benefits and costs of drinking and abstinence with the client. You will provide the client with additional information and present the rationale for the use of mindfulness in ERT. The client will learn that mindfulness is a skill that involves directing attention to either one thing, like an object or their breath, or to a broader attentional field to include noticing whatever they are experiencing in the present moment. Between-session skill practice will be assigned.

Session Outline

- Session introduction
- In-session exercise: Decisional Balance for Abstinence
- More about mindfulness
- Mindful Observing
- In-Session skill practice: Object-Centered Mindfulness
- Between-session skill practice

Session Introduction

Conduct Breathalyzer Test

Brief Mindfulness Exercise: Body Scan (3–5 Minutes)

> Each time we meet, we'll spend just a few minutes practicing mindfulness to get started. Last time, we did a mindfulness exercise called a Body Scan. I'd like to take a few minutes to do this again.

Brief Body Scan Script

Allow your eyes to gently close (or leave them slightly open if that is more comfortable). Place your feet on the floor, and let your body settle, relaxing into the chair, feeling the weight of your body on the chair...

Now taking a slow deep breath ... and "just noticing" whatever you may be feeling in your body ... becoming aware of any sensations you may be experiencing in the present moment.

Starting with your head, notice any physical sensations in your scalp ... ears ... eyes ... and mouth ... (5 seconds) shifting your attention down now to your jaw ... throat ... neck ... and noticing whatever is there ... or maybe feeling nothing in particular...

Bringing your awareness to your shoulders ... your back ... noting any sensations you are having ... Now tuning in to your stomach ... your chest ... following the sensations of your breath as it comes and goes ...

Feeling now into the upper arms ... lower arms ... and hands ... Now shifting your attention to your hips ... thighs ... knees ... (5 seconds) and noticing whatever is there...

Bringing awareness to your lower legs, feet. . and toes ... (5 seconds) Feeling your feet inside your shoes ... sensing the support of the floor beneath your shoes

Moving back up now, and building an awareness of your body as a whole ... the legs and hips ... stomach and chest ... shoulders, neck, and head ... (5 seconds) Noticing your body as a whole ... its sitting position ... how that feels...

Shifting your attention now to the sounds around you ...

Gently allowing your eyes to open ...

Review Between-Session Skill Practice

Reviewing the client's between-session skill practice conveys the *importance* of the assignment, identifies any *barriers* to skill practice, provides an opportunity to *positively reinforce* the client's effort, and identifies activities the client found *helpful*. You can begin the review with an open-ended question:

- *Last time we met, your plan was to practice the Body Scan for 5 minutes twice daily? How is that going?*
- *How about Stop and Notice?*

Collaborate with the client to problem solve any barriers that may have interfered with skill rehearsal.

- *What prevented you from carrying out your plan as you intended?*
- *Was there anything odd or confusing about the purpose of the skill?*
- *Was there any confusion about how to practice the skill?*

Session 2: Motivation and Mindfulness 55

If the client seems ambivalent about further skill practice, then review the rationale and see if the client can recommit to any amount of between-session skill practice. Consider breaking down the skill into smaller components to make it simpler and easier for the client to implement.

> **TIP** Asking permission before providing advice, direction, or education can help to decrease resistance and encourage a collaborative atmosphere. For example, *"Would it be okay if I shared some information about the benefits of skill practice?"*

In this treatment, we will continue to discuss a variety of skills, in particular ones that have been found by most people to be helpful in reaching the goal of abstinence. However, it is likely you will find some skills more helpful than others. Skill practice is an important part of learning a new skill, so we encourage regular practice. Ultimately, how much you practice is up to you. We do know that in order to determine whether a specific skill is helpful, it first must be attempted. The skills we have discussed so far are intended to help you develop a greater awareness of the present moment. Well-learned behaviors, like drinking, can be reflexive or automatic; they don't require much thought or effort. However, changing a well-learned behavior begins with greater awareness. The more awareness you have about your own habits, the easier it is to make and sustain changes. How does this sound to you? Looking ahead, what could you do this week to help you develop greater awareness?

Reinforce any attempt to practice between-session skills.

You identified both a time and place for doing the Body Scan and you practiced on three of the seven days since we last met. That's a good start!

Finally, identify aspects of the skill practice that the client found helpful.

- *What did you find helpful about your practice?*

Reinforce successful skill use and progress. This can be accomplished while reviewing the Daily Monitoring Log, if desired. Reinforce the client's use of other skills they may have used over the past week and progress toward or maintenance of abstinence.

Sample questions:

- *Any high-risk situations getting easier to manage?*
- *Were there times when you wanted to drink but didn't?*
- *How did you get through that situation without drinking?*

Review Daily Monitoring Log

The Daily Monitoring Log provides a record of the client's high-risk drinking situations and includes urges or cravings, daily alcohol use (in standard drink equivalents), and any skills or strategies used to cope with the situation. Probe for details in order to gain an understanding of the client's thoughts and emotions in these challenging situations.

Review the client's completed Daily Monitoring Log. If not completed, ask the client if they experienced any challenging situations since the last treatment session. Take a few minutes to explore situations in which the client reports having had a moderate or greater urge to drink. Ask if they were with others or alone, what they were doing at the time, and when and where they experienced the urge to drink. Have the client write this information on a blank monitoring log. Also ask the client to rate the strength of the urge in that situation and whether the urge was elicited by a positive or negative emotion. Ask whether they abstained or consumed alcohol. If they were successful in maintaining abstinence, which skills or strategies did they utilize? If they drank, how many standard drinks were consumed? Reinforce abstinence and use of any alcohol or emotion-specific coping skills.

Review Treatment Goals

Direct the client's attention to Chapter 3 of the client workbook that includes the prompt, "What I hope to gain from treatment." If this prompt was not completed, work with the client to complete it at this time.

> *Let's spend a few minutes on the* prompt, *"What I hope to gain from treatment." I see that you wrote* [summarize what the client wrote]. *Is there anything else you would like to add?*

Link client goals to skill-building and emotion regulation training:

> *Over the course of treatment, you will learn and practice a variety of skills that can help you achieve your goals. As you continue to build and practice these skills within and between sessions, you will find yourself better prepared to manage situations involving alcohol including situations involving unpleasant emotions. As we discussed previously, between-session practice and use of these skills is an important part of this treatment.*

A Different Path

The client may indicate a treatment goal for a problem that might not be feasible to address in this treatment. For example, ERT does not directly address marital or relationship problems. ERT can't "make their marriage better." However, if drinking has contributed to the client's marital distress, then addressing the drinking problem may have an indirect positive impact on the marital relationship. In addition, the therapist can provide a referral for marital counseling if the client would like one.

In-Session Exercise: Decisional Balance for Abstinence

Briefly introduce the decisional balance exercise. This exercise is intended to explore the benefits and costs of continuing to drink as usual and the benefits and costs of abstaining from alcohol. Begin by orienting the client to the "Weighing the Benefits and Costs of Drinking" section of Chapter 4 of the client workbook. Using the examples provided, begin reviewing the benefits of continuing to drink as usual and proceed in a clockwise direction with costs of continuing to drink, then costs of abstaining from alcohol and finally, end with benefits of abstaining from alcohol. This order is important because it leaves the client thinking about the benefits of abstinence. As you work through the example provided, the client is free to circle any benefits and costs that are true for them. After reviewing the example, continue the discussion by focusing on the client's perceived benefits and costs, following the same clockwise order.

Let's spend a few minutes looking at the possible benefits and costs of continuing to drink versus abstaining from alcohol. Let's begin with benefits of continuing to drink as usual. What benefits does drinking provide for you? What do you get from drinking? What are the costs of continuing to drink this way?

Let's switch gears now and talk about abstaining from alcohol. Tell me your thoughts about the costs of abstaining from drinking, what would the downsides be for you? Finally, tell me about the benefits of abstaining from alcohol. What do you stand to gain from being abstinent?

> **TIP** Make a copy of the client's Decisional Balance Worksheet to refer to in future sessions.

More About Mindfulness

> *Today, we will take time to expand your understanding of mindfulness. Why mindfulness?, you might wonder. How will it help you stop drinking? Well, as I have said before, our behavior is guided by thoughts, emotions, and physical sensations (e.g., we have an itch and we scratch it). When we engage in a behavior hundreds and thousands of time, we become very efficient at reacting to these internal experiences. We act or react quickly to internal (e.g., thoughts, urges) and external (e.g., people, places, things) cues often without much awareness. It's like being on autopilot. Mindfulness is a skill that you will learn that allows you to be less reactive to what is happening in the present moment. As you become a better observer of your own behavior, you gain the ability to make better choices including the choice to not drink.*
>
> *So what IS mindfulness? Last time, I asked "What comes to mind when you hear the word* mindfulness?*"*

Take a minute to review your discussion with the client during the prior session. Further explore and correct any misconceptions the client may have regarding the purpose or practice of mindfulness. For example, if the client equates mindfulness with meditation, and the client is not interested in meditation, then explain that while some people do practice mindfulness meditation, ERT does not require people to "meditate." Rather, ERT focuses on the application of mindfulness skills in everyday life. This is called *mindfulness* or "intentionally noticing whatever you experience in the present moment, with a mindset of mild curiosity or interest." If helpful, the words "on purpose" may be used instead of "intentionally." Prompt client for their thoughts on this definition.

> *That's right, when being mindful, you will switch out of autopilot mode and will learn to direct your attention to the "here and now."*
>
> *Think of it this way: If going through your usual day-to-day routine on autopilot is like being carried along by the current in a river, going wherever the current takes you, then being mindful is making a choice to get out of the river and climb onto shore. You are no longer going wherever the current takes you. Instead, you have pulled yourself out. Now you have a chance to see where you are, to observe the river's current rather than being swept away by it, and to choose your direction instead of it being chosen for you.*

> *That's what we are doing when we Stop and Notice. We stop floating along, and begin to take notice. That's one way of being mindful. Why is it important to Stop and Notice, to "hit pause"? What happens when we do this? Well, this technique creates an opportunity to do something different; it creates a space for change. Does this make sense?*

This presents an opportunity to guide a brief discussion with the client on how mindfulness allows us to slow things down and become aware of both internal sensations and external stimuli that we didn't previously notice. This also creates an opportunity for the client to do things differently.

> *Slowing down to notice your thoughts and feelings allows for the possibility of taking a different action or changing your behavior. For example, if you are speeding along a highway, you may not notice all of the signs and exits. However, when you slow down, it is easier to see each new sign and exit and then decide what you would like to do.*

> **TIP** The term "hit pause" is used purposely here in order to begin familiarizing the client with concepts that will be used later in treatment, during the direct experiencing of emotion sessions.

Mindful Observing

Mindful Observing is a more sustained version of "Stop and Notice." "Stop and Notice" is the first step, and occurs when the person switches out of autopilot and enters or "wakes up" to the present moment. Observing occurs when the person remains in the present moment; it's also described as "watching." Watching creates a space or distance between the watcher and what is being observed in the moment (i.e., an emotion, thought, or external event) thus decreasing the intensity of the experience and reactivity. The concept of distancing is usually easily understood by clients and has appeal for those who may be hesitant to engage with unpleasant thoughts, emotions, and sensations:

> *As you "Stop and Notice," then you can "take it to the next level" by "watching" or "observing" what you are noticing. You climb out of the river and onto the riverbank, sit down, and notice. And you keep noticing . . . things like _____ (mention something the client noticed*

either in session or during the between-session practice such as sounds, physical sensations, emotions, or thoughts). *You watch or observe these things as they come and go, watching from the riverbank, removed from the river itself. You've stepped back a bit, still noticing, but doing so from a short distance away. You cultivate a mindset of mild interest, or curiosity. If you could "hear" this mindset, it might sound something like this,* (Speak in a mildly curious, nonjudgmental tone of voice) *"Hmm . . . I'm noticing this kind of hungry feeling . . . where do I notice it? What does it feel like? . . . (5 seconds) I'm noticing thoughts about eating . . . Where could I get something quick . . . maybe that hamburger place? . . . (5 seconds) But do I want to spend the money? . . .* (therapist to self in kind, nonjudgmental tone of voice) *whoops! Stay on the bank . . . okay, noticing . . . watching . . . thinking about money now . . .* (therapist sighs) *. . . I'm sighing . . . What's that feel like?"*

Does this make sense? Ensure that client understands the intent of the Mindful Observing stance.

When you are noticing or observing, you can watch whatever goes by such as thoughts, emotions, physical sensations, anything at all. You can also decide to watch or notice something more specific. With the Body Scan, you are turning your attention specifically toward physical sensations. Today, I'd like to do an exercise that starts by observing or watching whatever you are noticing in the moment, and then turns your attention specifically to an object.

In-Session Skill Practice: Object-Centered Mindfulness

This exercise directs the client to focus attention on the rich and numerous details of one object. Object-centered mindfulness, therefore, involves a narrowing of the client's attention. At the end of this exercise, the client will be directed to broaden the focus of attention, or "zoom out," to cultivate awareness of other elements of the present moment such as thoughts, emotions, and physical sensations.

Adapt the script that follows as needed, taking into account the nature of the object and what would work best for the client.

> **TIP** This script contains a number of questions that are intended to prompt various ways in which the client can explore the object. To maximize the client's present-focused sensory experience, and minimize the involvement of interpersonal interactions, read questions as though they were statements, without raising the pitch or intonation of your voice at the end. You may notice that some questions and phrases are not punctuated by a question mark, and this is by design.

Session 2: Motivation and Mindfulness 61

Offer the client a choice of objects to select from and use during this exercise. We have found that polished and rough cut stones are popular with clients and inexpensive. However, other objects may be used effectively, even something as common as a paper clip. The object can be given to client to take home for between-session skill practice.

Ask the client to place the object on a nearby table or in the palm of their hand, if no surface is available. Let the client know that they will be guided through the exercise and that there will be some brief silences during the exercise during which they can continue to center attention on the object or elsewhere, as guided. The therapist then guides the Object-Centered Mindfulness exercise using the following script:

Take a few slow deep breaths, bringing yourself to the present moment . . . (Model slow deep breaths without pausing or holding the breath between the inhale and exhale, for the client to follow, taking about 10–15 seconds.)

Take a few moments to really look at this (object). Look at it as if you have never seen anything like this before, like this is the first time . . .

What do you notice about it . . .

What do you notice when you look at the surface . . . Is it smooth . . . bumpy . . . rough . . .

What about its shape . . . Its edges . . .

Are there any shadows . . . Where are they . . . What do the edges of the shadows look like . . . Are they clear and distinct, fuzzy or blurred . . .

Move your head slightly so different parts of it come into view. What do you notice . . . Watching any changes . . .

Now reach out and touch it. What do you notice . . . Do you feel the pressure on your fingers . . .

Move your fingers over the surface. What does it feel like . . . What is the temperature like . . .

Move the object slightly, watching what happens . . . Do the shadows change . . . Can you hear any sound . . .

Pick it up with your fingers . . . (If it is held in the palm, pick it up with the other hand.)

Turn it over (or around), and look at it from different angles, watching the details shift . . . Noticing how it feels where it comes in contact with your skin . . .

Slowly place it into the palm of your hand, feeling its weight . . . What else do you notice . . .

Slightly move your hand, watching what happens . . . Does it (the object) move . . . How does it feel against your skin as your hand moves . . .

Softly close your hand around it, and slowly drop your hand, until it is resting comfortably. Gently allow your eyes to close . . . and bring your attention to the sense of the body breathing . . . each

> *breath coming and going as it will, not having to breathe any certain way . . . (about 10 seconds)*
>
> *And letting your attention expand beyond the breath to the entire body . . . curious . . . noticing any sensations in the body . . . (about 10 seconds)*
>
> *Shifting your attention now to sounds . . . not trying to listen, but just noticing whatever sounds come into your awareness . . . (about 10 seconds)*
>
> *Gently allowing your eyes to open . . .*

Following completion of the exercise, process the client's experience using some or all of the following prompts:

> *What did you notice? (e.g., colors, texture, weight) What was that like? What else did you notice (e.g., emotions, thoughts, memories, liking the object)? You may have noticed your mind wandering during this mindfulness exercise. Minds can be like puppies—they get distracted by things and quickly wander off to explore. It's important to remember that this is perfectly normal! Wandering is what minds do; it's not a mistake or a sign that you are not "good" at mindfulness. If this happens while you are practicing mindfulness exercises in your daily life, don't be concerned. Just noticing that your attention has drifted is being mindful. All you need to do is gently center your attention back on the object.*

If the client reports remaining focused during the exercise, mention that they may notice their mind wandering more often when they engage in mindfulness practice between sessions.

Address any barriers to mindfulness practice mentioned by the client. See information on Common Barriers to Mindfulness Practice in Appendix A.

Between-Session Skill Practice

- Practice Dedicated Mindfulness: Object-Centered Mindfulness exercise for five minutes twice daily.
- Practice Mindful Observing during daily activities four times per day.
- Complete the Daily Monitoring Log.
- Optional—add additional costs and benefits to Weighing the Benefits and Costs of Drinking worksheet.

Making It Happen

- Build it into daily life.
- Think about when and where to rehearse skills.
- Use cues to remember to practice the skills.

Chapter 6

Session 3
High-Risk Situations and Mindful Coping

Materials

Managing Negative Emotions Without Drinking workbook, Chapter 5
Managing Negative Emotions Without Drinking workbook, Chapter 4 Session Highlights: A Note About Wandering Minds
Therapist Brief Object-Centered Mindfulness Script
Therapist Mindful Breathing Script

Session Overview

In this session you will review common high-risk drinking situations and begin to identify the client's personal high-risk situations. Emotional education regarding the role of maladaptive coping strategies for managing emotions such as suppression, avoidance, and escape, and the advantages of adaptive strategies that involve engaging with uncomfortable emotions and cravings or urges to drink alcohol will be presented to the client. The relationship of unpleasant emotions to alcohol consumption will be discussed. In addition, the skills of Watch the Wave, Mindful Breathing, and Name the Emotion are introduced to continue building awareness and provide a strategy for managing and regulating emotions and urges to drink. Informal mindfulness practice, referred to as Mindful Moments, is discussed.

Session Outline

- Session introduction
- High-risk situations
- The problem with avoidance and suppression
- Emotion regulation skills: Watch the Wave, Breathe Mindfully, Mindful Moments, Name the Emotion
- Between-session skill practice

Session Introduction

Conduct Breathalyzer Test

Brief Mindfulness Exercise: Object-Centered Mindfulness (3–5 Minutes)

This session's brief mindfulness exercise will reinforce the between-session skill practice of object-centered mindfulness, and briefly incorporate the breath as well as an opportunity to practice attention shifting from a narrow focus (the object) to a broader, more inclusive awareness of the present moment.

In ERT, we use polished stones of various colors and dimensions as the object of choice for this exercise. Ask the client to hold the stone in the palm of their hand and then proceed with the following script.

> *Brief Object-Centered Mindfulness Script*
>
> *Take a few slow deep breaths and bring yourself to the present moment. Take a few moments to examine this stone. Look at it closely. Notice its shape. Its surface. Feel the surface. Sense its weight.*
>
> *Now close your hand around it and observe the changes in what the stone feels like in your hand. Now open your hand and set the stone down and rest comfortably in your chair.*
>
> *Close your eyes and bring your attention to the physical sensation of your breath. Notice how it feels for each breath as it comes and goes. And with your breath in the background, let your attention expand to your entire body, becoming aware of any sensations in the body.*
>
> *Shift your attention now to sounds, the breath still in the background . . . not trying to listen, but just noticing whatever sounds come into your awareness . . . (10 seconds)*
>
> *Bring your attention back to your breath, feeling the body as a whole as the breath comes and goes (10 seconds) . . . and gently allow your eyes to open.*

Review Between-Session Skill Practice

Work collaboratively with the client to problem solve any barriers that may have interfered with skill practice. If the client is experiencing difficulties, see Chapter 3 of this guide for ways to increase client engagement with between-session skill practice.

Reinforce Other Successful Skill Use and Progress

Highlight successful skill use and progress toward (or maintenance of) abstinence. If the client was successful in maintaining abstinence, ask what they did to refrain from drinking. That is, which methods or skills did they utilize? If the situation involved an unpleasant emotion, how did they attempt to manage it? If abstinent, reinforce the success. If they drank, what amount was consumed? The Daily Monitoring Log provides valuable information regarding high-risk situations, and provides an opportunity for both you and the client to highlight successes as well as to troubleshoot situations that continue to present a challenge for remaining abstinent.

Review Daily Monitoring Log

Review the client's Daily Monitoring Log. If the client has not completed it, take a few minutes to explore situations in which the client reports having had a moderate or greater urge to drink. Ask if they were with others or alone, what they were doing at the time, and when and where they experienced the urge to drink. Have the client write this information on a blank monitoring log. Also ask the client to rate the strength of the urge in that situation and whether the urge was elicited by a positive or negative emotion. Ask whether they abstained or consumed alcohol. If they were successful in maintaining abstinence, which methods or skills did they utilize? If they drank, how many standard drinks were consumed? Reinforce abstinence and use of any alcohol and/or emotion-specific coping skills.

Provide feedback on the skills or strategies that the client used since the last session including the effectiveness of the skills. This includes suggesting a different skill or set of skills that the client can use in the situation. This is particularly important for more difficult high-risk situations that may pose a unique challenge to the client, or that require additional attention. Enquire about any upcoming events that may be used for discussion of high-risk situations later in this session.

High-Risk Situations

Managing situations in which there is a high risk for alcohol use is an important skill for maintaining abstinence. High-risk situations are defined as those that present the highest risk for drinking, that is, those situations in which a person is most likely to drink. These situations can vary between individuals; engaging the client in a discussion can assist in identifying their personal high-risk situations:

> A high-risk drinking situation can be any situation which increases the likelihood of drinking. It doesn't have to be a specific event or place; it could be a certain time of day, or a long stretch of time with nothing to do. A high-risk drinking situation may also involve other people. When you're with a certain person or group of people there is a strong chance that you will drink. Once we know more about these situations, including any thoughts or emotions that you may have in these situations, we can begin to find ways to help you manage these situations without drinking. Also,

you may have your own effective strategies for managing these situations without the use of alcohol. If so, I would be interested to hear about them.

Explore Client's High-Risk Situations

Direct the client to the High-Risk Situations and Coping Plan worksheet in the client workbook. Begin by discussing the client's current high-risk drinking situations. Ask the client about their most frequent high-risk drinking situations. It is not necessary to engage in a thorough exploration of all drinking triggers. Make a note of those situations that involve an unpleasant emotion as you can refer back to these when discussing emotion regulation skills later in this session. Use one or more of the following questions to prompt a discussion of the client's high-risk situations:

- *What are some high-risk drinking situations for you?*
- *In what situations do you notice an increased desire or urge to drink?*
- *Where are you most likely to drink?*
- *When are you most likely to drink? What time of day, or days of the week?*
- *When is it hardest for you not to drink?*
- *Who are you most likely to have a drink with?*

A Different Path

Difficulty Identifying High-Risk Drinking Situations

Some clients may have difficulty identifying with the concept of a high-risk drinking situation. They may report drinking daily for a long period of time, or that they drink "all day" and have difficulty identifying any one event. Others may report that they "just drink" with little awareness of internal or external cues or triggering events. With these clients, the following prompts can be useful:

- *When do you usually drink? Where does this typically take place?*
- *Is there a time of day, or situation, during which you would never drink?*
- *Are there abstinent days? Days when you do not have any alcohol?*

When general questions fail, specific questions may help identify the client's high-risk situations. The reporter's adage regarding the five W's may be useful—who, what, where, when, and why. For example, has the client's drinking in the past been associated with particular events, places, or certain people? Did drinking frequently occur after an argument with a friend or spouse? Was it limited to paydays? If these questions still don't result in the identification of specific high-risk situations, then you will have promoted in the client an initial awareness of the types of cues that are often associated with drinking.

Review Common High-Risk Situations

Review the categories of common high-risk situations listed below to identify any additional situations. This review need not go into depth about each type of common high-risk situation. Instead, expand on specific categories only as needed. During the review, it can be helpful to mention the client's previously identified high-risk situations as examples when appropriate. Drinking-related thoughts will be explored in greater depth in Session 4, therefore limit the time spent discussing the influence of thoughts on drinking in this session.

Common high-risk situations include:

- Seeing alcohol or other people drinking
- People, places, times of day, and situations commonly associated with drinking (such as drinking buddies, parties and bars, getting home from work, weekends) or an opportunity to use alcohol without others knowing about it
- Unpleasant (e.g., frustration, fatigue, feeling stressed out) and pleasant emotions (e.g., elation, excitement, feelings of accomplishment)
- Increased thoughts about alcohol such as how good it would feel to drink, thinking about how to get the alcohol, or remembering times you used alcohol in the past.

In general, drinking is often related to what's going on around you, like the sight of alcohol or being around other people who are drinking. Emotions, such as stress, frustration, boredom, and also joy and excitement are often associated with drinking. Finally, thoughts, such as "I've had a hard day" or "I deserve a drink," can elicit an urge or desire to drink.

68 Session 3: High-Risk Situations

> *Let's go through this list one category at a time and you can tell me about your experience with these situations, and which ones are most often associated with drinking for you.*

The Problem With Avoidance and Suppression of Negative Emotions

Situations involving emotions are very common high-risk situations. Unpleasant emotions are often identified as reasons for drinking as well as reasons why people might return to their unhealthy drinking patterns. In this treatment, we focus on uncomfortable emotions, physical sensations, and cravings related to your use of alcohol. Let's take the next part of our session to continue building skills in this area.

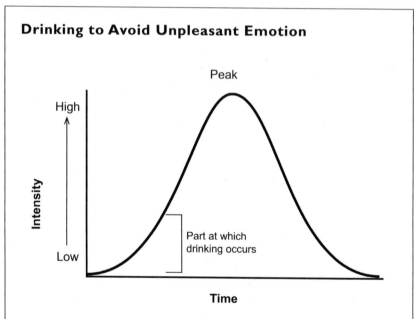

Figure 2 Emotion and Craving Over Time Wave

Figure 2 illustrates the time course of an unpleasant emotional response. Notice how drinking occurs at a lower level of emotional intensity and well in advance of the peak level of discomfort. By drinking early on in the development of the unpleasant emotional response, the person effectively avoids experiencing more intense levels of negative affect.

> *Let's begin with a review of the relationship between emotions and drinking.*

Session 3: High-Risk Situations

Emotions are very much like a wave. That is, they rise in intensity, reach a peak, and then subside. This may sound familiar; we've mentioned it briefly in previous sessions. The desire to drink, whether it comes in the form of thoughts, urges, or cravings, is very similar. It builds to a peak, and then subsides, just like a wave.

Having an urge to drink when you've decided not to drink, continuing to want the drink when you know it will end up causing problems for you such as _____ (insert client example of negative consequences of drinking), well, that's not something we would say is pleasant. The same can be said for uncomfortable emotions. We don't necessarily want to feel them—we'd rather they just go away. So, we push them back down, and maybe use alcohol to numb or escape from them. This works in the moment; the emotions, urges, or cravings decrease. The problem, however, is that they return and can be much more intense.

There are many research studies demonstrating that when we try to avoid, suppress, or push away uncomfortable emotions, they just keep coming back. This also holds true for thoughts and urges to drink. In fact, attempts to suppress or avoid urges and unpleasant emotions are often followed by "rebound" effects. Rebound effects may be experienced as more intense. For example, attempts to suppress an urge may produce stronger and more frequent urges.

A well-known research study used the "white bear" test to demonstrate this. They asked people not to think about a white bear. If a thought about a white bear arose, they were instructed to suppress it, push it away. Can you guess what happened?

Right. The thought kept coming back. The same thing happens with our emotions and unwanted thoughts. Some people describe it like "trying to hold back a waterfall."

Similarly, when alcohol is used to avoid or escape from an uncomfortable thought, emotion, or craving, it may be effective in the short term, but in the long run the uncomfortable experiences return. Not only do they return, but also each time someone uses alcohol to avoid or escape discomfort, whether it is an unpleasant emotion or a strong desire or craving to drink, the drinking response or behavior is reinforced. This makes it more likely that the drinking behavior will be repeated and the urge to drink more difficult to resist the next time.

Uncomfortable emotion → Drink alcohol → Relief from uncomfortable emotion → MORE LIKELY TO DRINK NEXT TIME

In this way, drinking to reduce discomfort is not that different from other actions that people take to reduce discomfort. A person has a headache, they take a pain reliever and the headache goes away. Next time they get a headache? Right, the person takes a pain reliever. Or, you start your car, you hear an annoying beeping or buzzing sound, you put your seat belt on, and the annoying sound stops. Next time? Yes, the seat belt goes on. Sometimes we put the seat belt on even before the annoying sound begins. We become very efficient at avoiding discomfort, taking action even before the discomfort begins.

 A Different Path

The client doesn't connect unpleasant emotions to drinking because drinking occurs in advance of unpleasant emotions.

The therapist may use the example of a person with social anxiety to demonstrate how, over time, the "escape" behavior of leaving a social event occurs earlier and earlier, eventually "backing up" to the point where the person avoids social events. This is an example of someone who has become very good, or efficient, at reducing and avoiding discomfort. The same process can happen when alcohol is used to escape from or reduce unpleasant emotions. The drinking behavior occurs earlier and earlier in the sequence of events, until the unpleasant emotion is avoided entirely.

> *Let's take the example of someone who gets anxious at social gatherings. Maybe the person decides to leave early to reduce their anxiety. As soon as they decide to leave, they feel some relief from the anxiety. Once they are gone, they feel even more relief. (The therapist then demonstrates this principle with a drinking situation.)*

The process is the same with alcohol. Each time an unpleasant emotion is reduced or eliminated by consuming alcohol, the drinking behavior is strengthened and reinforced.

If you think about the number of times you have experienced this process, the behavior of drinking has been reinforced many times over. To weaken the connection between unpleasant emotions and drinking, ERT teaches you a set of skills that you can use to manage your unpleasant emotions without the use of alcohol.

So, what can we do to help regulate and manage these uncomfortable emotions? Well, one very effective strategy involves directly experiencing the emotion. Have you heard the advice about what someone should do if they fall off a horse? Or fall off a bike?

(The client will typically respond that "you have to get right back on.")

> Right, we need to face it rather than avoid it. If we avoid the horse or the bike, our fear of those things will remain. In order to overcome the fear, we need to experience our uncomfortable emotions while remaining safe and without being "swept away" or overwhelmed by them. How does that sound to you?

Emotion Regulation Skills

Watch the Wave

> Last time, we introduced the idea of "watching" or observing what we are experiencing from moment to moment. We can notice and observe things that we see, touch, or hear through our senses, like when you focused on one object. We can also observe or watch our inner experiences like physical sensations, thoughts, and emotions. This is a mindfulness skill, just watching or observing whatever we are experiencing in the moment. Being an observer means we have stepped back a bit from what is happening and what we are experiencing in the moment. Observing in the moment with this little bit of space is different than suppressing or pushing uncomfortable feelings and unwanted thoughts away. They are still there, we notice them and are aware of them, but they just don't seem as powerful or overwhelming as they did before. When we apply this skill to our emotions, we are no longer trying to make them go away or suppress them. Instead we note their presence and watch as they come and go from the perspective of an observer, having put a little space between what we are observing and ourselves.
>
> Remember that emotions and urges are like waves. They're always changing. As you observe or watch them change, you will see how they start small, reach a peak, and then subside. This skill has been used for many years as a way to "ride out" an urge to drink, and is called "Urge Surfing." Urge Surfing also involves "tuning in" to notice the urge, and what it's like, rather than trying to suppress it. You can do this with emotions and the desire or urge to drink.

Breathe Mindfully

> As we've discussed, in being mindful, we deliberately pay attention to what is happening in the present moment. As we build this skill, we are increasingly aware of our thoughts, emotions, physical sensations,

72 Session 3: High-Risk Situations

Figure 3 Find Calm Below the Surface

cravings, and urges as they occur, and can ride them out as they come and go. We no longer have to react automatically in the same old way every time our buttons get pushed. Instead, this kind of awareness gives us more control over our actions, and that includes drinking. I'd like to tell you about a specific mindfulness technique. It is a way to build your skill of staying in the present moment, while at the same time helping you feel more "settled" when you want to manage or cope with uncomfortable feelings. Would that be okay with you?

Mindful Breathing is just what it sounds like—noticing your breathing. Unlike other kinds of breathing exercises, you don't have to breathe in a certain kind of way. The idea is to just notice your breath as it comes and goes.

With Mindful Breathing, we allow ourselves to be aware of thoughts and emotions, noticing them, watching and observing them, while staying in the present moment, using our breathing as an anchor. If you are "watching the wave," you can broaden your attention to include the breath.

You can practice Mindful Breathing at other times as well. When any uncomfortable thoughts, sensations, or emotions enter into your field of awareness while focusing on the breath, the response is to "just notice" them with a mindset of mild interest or curiosity, not judgment. Then "breathe with them and through them" neither pushing them away or clinging to them. Like the choppy surface of the ocean,

Session 3: High-Risk Situations   73

the mind can become agitated in reaction to a difficult situation. Below the ocean surface, there is only gentle swelling (Figure 3). As we focus on our breathing at the belly (or stomach, or abdomen), we remain calmer and have more control over our actions.

In-Session Skill Practice: Mindful Breathing

Working collaboratively, engage the client in a Mindful Breathing exercise. This exercise should take about 10 minutes:

> *Most people find Mindful Breathing to be relaxing and pleasant. What do you think? Would you like to give it a try? Okay, I'll read this guided Mindful Breathing exercise to you, and you'll just follow along. Let's start by getting comfortable.*
>
> *Place both feet flat on the floor. Do something comfortable with your hands. Sit with your back, neck, and head in good alignment. Sit in a way that promotes alertness and wakefulness. Let your eyes close gently. Notice your feet on the floor, your back against the chair, your hands resting where they are, and your face and head where they are. Allow yourself to feel the heaviness of your body. Allow yourself to relax into the support of the chair and the floor beneath you. Let your body ease and settle as much as possible.*
>
> *Bring attention to your stomach. Allow it to relax and become soft. Let it stay soft. Focus on the sensation of your breath as it comes and goes. Focus your attention at the place in your own body where you can feel your breath come and go most easily and naturally. For some this is the abdomen, for others the chest, and for others the nose or even the mouth, if you tend to breathe with your mouth open. Let your attention settle and focus exactly on that place where the breath sensations are easiest for you to feel. If you aren't sure exactly where to focus, the abdomen is a good place to start. Let your attention rest there now. Allow yourself to feel the sensation of the breath moving in and out of the body just as it is.*
>
> *Allow the breath to come and go without interfering or trying to control it. This practice is about strengthening your attention and awareness, not controlling the breath. Keep the focus on just this breath. Let go of any thoughts about how many breaths or the next breath or the last breath. Just this breath. If it helps you to focus, you could whisper quietly to yourself "in" on the in breath, "out" on the out breath, and "pause" or "space" for the space between the breaths. Try to remain present for the entire cycle of each breath: in, out, pause, in, out, and so on. As your attention strengthens and mindfulness grows, you can begin to notice the beginning of the "in" breath, the middle, and the end. You can do the same for the "out" breath.*

> Let your attention settle more deeply into the variety of sensations of the breath in the body. Allow the feeling of the rise and fall of the abdominal wall, the actual stretching sensation, to be the focus. Notice the changing patterns of sensation, how each breath is different—some shallow, some deep, some strong, some weak, some choppy, some smooth. Meet each breath as if sensing it for the first time. In truth, each breath is here once and only once. Welcome it.
>
> When your attention wanders away from the breath, gently notice where it went. It could be a thought, or a sound outside. No matter where your mind wanders, with patience and kindness, bring your attention gently back to the place in the body where you are concentrating on your breathing. Praise yourself for noticing that your attention has wandered. This is what minds do. Recognizing when the mind wanders is a moment of mindfulness. It is a part of becoming more present in the moment.
>
> As you continue to focus on your breathing, keep your belly soft. Notice if there is tightening and tension in the body. Allow softening and relaxing as much as possible. Keep practicing this way for a few more minutes. If you notice feelings such as restlessness, boredom, fear, anxiety, or sleepiness building and demanding your attention, gently notice that. Notice any tendency to fight them. Try to let them be and return your attention to your breathing. Okay, you can open your eyes now and stretch if you like. Notice how you feel, and then let that feeling go.

Process the client's experience. Example prompts include:

- *What was that like for you?*
- *What did you notice?*
- *Was any part difficult or confusing?*
- *How are you feeling?*

Mindful Moments

At this point in the session, you will discuss informal mindfulness practices with the client. In Session 1 you discussed with the client formal or Dedicated Mindfulness such as the Body Scan activity. As an alternative to formal mindfulness, which requires the client to set aside time during the day to practice, informal practice can be completed most anytime during the client's day. These informal mindfulness practices, which we refer to as Mindful Moments, can increase moment-to-moment awareness and can be an effective means for managing unpleasant emotions and urges and cravings.

Previously, we talked about how mindfulness allows you to slow things down and become more aware of what's happening in the present moment. Increased awareness allows for the possibility of doing something different. In our first session, we discussed Dedicated Mindfulness, which requires you to set aside time during the day to practice. Today, we are going to talk about ways to be mindful as you are going about your day-to-day activities. We refer to these informal mindfulness practices as Mindful Moments. These are all strategies for managing emotions and urges and cravings in the moment.

Name the Emotion

Being able to describe how we feel is essential for regulating and managing our emotions. Although we can't always choose what emotions to feel or when to feel them, by developing emotional awareness, we may have greater flexibility in how we choose to respond to what we're feeling.

The more aware you are of what emotions you are feeling, the better you will be at regulating them. The process of figuring out which words best describe our emotions leads to greater awareness, insight, and clarity. As our understanding of what we're feeling and why we're feeling it comes into focus, we then can plan more effective ways to respond. Labeling our emotions provides us with greater flexibility in how we choose to respond to what we're feeling. Putting a label or name on something often removes the confusion and uncertainty that can come with the "unknown." What was once hazy or unclear becomes clear and distinct.

Society doesn't often encourage the skill of labeling emotions, so many people find themselves unable to identify how they feel. "Fine," "great" "okay" "not great" . . . these terms are not specific enough to be helpful for regulating emotions, although they can be a good place to start. Fortunately, just choosing more specific words from the Emotions List can quickly expand a person's emotion vocabulary. Even if you can't seem to find a word that fits "perfectly," this process of considering which words might describe what we are feeling is still effective for helping us regulate our emotions.

Between-Session Skill Practice

Dedicated Mindfulness

Don't be surprised if your Mindful Breathing seems different when you practice between sessions. Because your mindfulness practice will be self-guided, you might find that your attention drifts from the focus on your breath. When this happens, notice that your mind has wandered and gently bring your attention back to the breath. There is more information about this topic in your workbook.

Point out the location of "A Note About Wandering Minds" (see client workbook, Chapter 4).

- Have the client practice Mindful Breathing for 3–5 minutes twice daily.

Mindful Moments

In the previous sessions, "Stop and Notice" and Observing were introduced. Now both of these skills will be incorporated into daily informal mindfulness practice. Collaborate with the client to select one or two daily activities that they can mindfully observe.

- Have the client engage in a Mindful Moment, several times per day.

Watch the Wave

Try "watching the wave" when you have an urge to drink. Watch and observe any emotions, thoughts, or physical sensations you experience in an interested and "gentle" way. Make a conscious choice not to act on any urges to drink. Notice what is happening in your body and in your mind, not reacting, just watching the urge as it rises, peaks, and then subsides.

Name the Emotion

You and the client will decide on a manageable goal for Naming the Emotion using the Daily Monitoring Log. For example, if the client has not written down any emotions, perhaps a goal of naming one emotion on the upcoming week's self-monitoring log would be an appropriate goal.

- Continue Daily Monitoring Log.
- Continue adding high-risk situations to the High-Risk Situations and Coping Plan worksheet.

Making It Happen

- Build it into daily life.
- Think about when and where to rehearse skills.
- Use reminders or cues to practice the skills.

Chapter 7

Session 4
Drinking-Related Thoughts, Coping With Urges and Cravings, and Cognitive Reappraisal

Materials

Managing Negative Emotions Without Drinking workbook, Chapter 6
Therapist Brief Mindful Breathing Script, located in this chapter

Session Overview

This session will review the role of thoughts in increasing risk for drinking. Coping skills for managing drinking-related thoughts will be reviewed. Next, the client will learn about Cognitive Reappraisal and the therapist will discuss the impact of using Cognitive Reappraisal for managing emotions that increase risk for drinking.

Session Outline

- Session introduction
- Drinking-related thoughts and coping skills
- Managing emotions with Cognitive Reappraisal
- In-session skill practice: applying skills to a negative emotion drinking situation
- Between-session skill practice

Session Introduction

Conduct Breathalyzer Test

Brief Mindfulness Exercise (3–5 Minutes)

Using the following script, introduce the client to the Mindful Breathing exercise. This is one of several mindfulness exercises covered in this treatment.

> *If you recall, we will spend a few minutes at the beginning of each session practicing a mindfulness exercise. Last time, we focused*

mindfully on the breath. Today I'd like to take a few minutes to do a brief version of Mindful Breathing.

Mindful Breathing Script

Place both feet flat on the floor. Do something comfortable with your hands. Sit with your back, neck, and head in good alignment.

Let your eyes close gently. Notice your feet on the floor, your back against the chair, your hands resting where they are, and your face and head where they are. Allow yourself to feel the heaviness of your body. Allow yourself to relax and ease into the support of the chair and the floor beneath you.

Bring attention to your stomach. Allow it to relax, and focus on the sensation of your breath as it comes and goes. Focus your attention at the place in your own body where you can feel your breath come and go most easily and naturally. Let your attention settle and rest exactly on that place where the breath sensations are easiest for you to feel.

Allow yourself to feel the sensation of the breath moving in and out of the body just as it is. Allow the breath to come and go without interfering or trying to control it. This practice is about strengthening your attention and awareness, not controlling the breath. Keep the focus on just this breath.

Try to remain present for the entire cycle of each breath: in, out . . . in, out, in, out . . . Let your attention settle more deeply into the variety of sensations of the breath in the body. Notice the changing patterns of sensation, how each breath is different.

Just notice any other feelings, thoughts, sounds, or other sensations that enter into your field of awareness. Notice if there is tightening and tension in the body. Try to let them be and return your attention to your breathing.

Okay, you can open your eyes.

Review Between-Session Skill Practice

Work collaboratively with the client to problem solve any barriers that may have interfered with skill practice. If the client is experiencing difficulties, see Chapter 3 of this guide for ways to increase client engagement with between-session skill practice.

Highlight Skill Use and Progress

Review with the client the use of skills in high-risk-for-drinking situations including their progress toward the goal of abstinence.

Sample questions include:

- *Are there skills that you were able to use this week to keep you on track with your goal of abstinence?*

- Any high-risk situations getting easier to manage?
- Were there times when you wanted to drink but didn't?

Review Daily Monitoring Log

Review the client's completed Daily Monitoring Log. If the client has not completed the log, spend a few minutes reviewing one or two situations during the past week in which the client had a moderate or greater urge to drink. Provide encouragement for completing the log, stressing the importance of the information for understanding and "troubleshooting" high-risk situations. If the client was successful in maintaining abstinence, reinforce this success and explore the use of skills in these situations. If the client drank, what amount was consumed? Pay particular attention to situations involving negative affect. Probe for additional details regarding the client's most frequent or most difficult high-risk situations.

Sample questions include:

- *How have things been going? . . . Were there times when you wanted to drink?*
- *Let's look over the self-monitoring log . . . What were some ratings for your desire to drink?*
- *Is this a situation in which you tried to abstain? What did you do (skills or strategies) to get through it without drinking?*
- *How well did this work?*
- *Tell me about your drinking.*
- *How many standard drinks did you have on that day?*

Provide feedback on the skills or strategies used since the last session including the effectiveness of the skills. Suggest any additional skills, or modifications to skills used, that might be useful in the particular high-risk drinking situations. Highlight difficult or frequent high-risk situations that may require additional skills or strategies. Ask the client about any upcoming situations that could pose potential difficulties for them.

Drinking-Related Thoughts and Coping Skills

Today we'll take a closer look at how thoughts influence our behavior. The goal is to increase awareness of the kinds of thoughts that may lead to drinking and to learn effective ways to manage these thoughts. Remember, the goal is not to keep you from having these thoughts about drinking—thoughts about drinking are normal. It is really about changing your behavior when you have these thoughts. By changing how you respond to these thoughts, you create an opportunity to gain more control over your actions.

Notice Drinking-Related Thoughts

Direct the client's attention to the information sheet, "Thoughts That May Lead to Drinking," found in Chapter 6 of the client workbook. Engage the client in a discussion of which thoughts they commonly experience:

> *This is a list of common types of thoughts that could lead to drinking. Do you find yourself having any of these kinds of thoughts? Which ones are most common? The more you notice these thoughts when they cross your mind, the more likely you are to make a conscious and informed choice about how you want to respond to them.*

Coping Skills

Direct the client's attention to the section, "Coping With Thoughts, Cravings, and Urges," found in Chapter 6 of the client workbook. Explain to the client that the desire to drink can come in several forms and briefly review the following information. Use the analogy of a stray cat to support abstaining from alcohol.

> *In addition to drinking thoughts, people can also experience the desire to drink as a craving or an urge. The desire to drink is like a stray cat. If you feed it by drinking, it will keep coming back. If you don't feed it, it will eventually stay away.*

As you review the Coping With Thoughts, Cravings and Urges information sheet, ask the client which of the coping skills they prefer for coping with the thoughts:

Thoughts, cravings, and urges to drink:

- *May be unwanted and uncomfortable, but are common and normal, and don't mean something is wrong.*
- *Occur more often earlier in treatment. The desire to drink gets easier to manage as abstinence continues.*
- *Are time-limited. The desire to drink will pass with time.*
- *Are weakened when you get through them without drinking. Each time you let them pass without drinking, your ability to manage them effectively is strengthened.*

The following coping skills are helpful for coping with drinking thoughts as well as cravings and urges:

1. Avoid, leave, or change the situation

   Avoid, leave, or change situations in which you start thinking about or wanting to drink. Try a different activity such as exercise or a hobby.

Try getting rid of alcohol in the house, not going to parties or bars, reducing contact with friends who drink, and so on. This is especially helpful early in the recovery process. However, avoiding people and places has its limitations. The use of alcohol is woven into the fabric of our society, making it impossible to avoid alcohol completely. Alcohol and reminders about alcohol such as billboards and commercials seem to be everywhere. Trying to avoid them completely would be very difficult and limiting. For those times when you are unable to avoid, leave, or change the situation, you will need other ways to manage your thoughts or desire to drink.

2. **Challenge the thoughts**

    Use other thoughts to challenge the drinking thoughts. We can use different thoughts to challenge thoughts about drinking. For example, if the thought is "I need a drink to wind down right now," challenge the thought with this comeback "I don't have to drink to unwind; I can unwind another way, like watching my favorite shows."

3. **Remember why**

    Initiate a brief discussion with the client regarding the benefits of not drinking and the negative consequences of drinking. Have the client refer to the previously completed decisional balance exercise. Provide the client with a 3 × 5 inch lined notecard to record the benefits of not drinking and the negative consequences of drinking.

    Many people have a tendency to remember only the positive effects of alcohol and often forget the unpleasant experiences or negative consequences of drinking. When having drinking thoughts many people find it helpful to remind themselves of the benefits of not drinking and the negative consequences of drinking. This way, you can remind yourself that you really won't "feel better if you just have one drink," and that you stand to lose a lot by drinking. Let's brainstorm some of the benefits of not drinking and the negative consequences of drinking. I have a notecard for you on which you can write these down.

4. **Eat, snack, or drink something nonalcoholic**

    Another effective way to manage thoughts and cravings to drink is by having a good meal, snack, or a nonalcoholic drink. Most people do not feel like drinking alcoholic beverages after eating a big meal or something very sweet. At times, feeling thirsty for a drink may be more about needing hydration rather than a true desire for alcohol.

5. **Self-reinforcement**

    It's easy for people to become focused on things that didn't turn out well. But you don't want these difficulties to overshadow your successes. So, it can be helpful to remind yourself of your successes. This can include being successful in remaining abstinent in your usual drinking situations, using a newly learned skill, or managing difficulties in a way that doesn't involve drinking.

6. Decision delay

    Put off the decision to drink for 15 minutes. This provides the opportunity for thoughts and urges to drink to come and go. If you wait a while, you may find that the desire to drink passes.

 A Different Path

Most clients will be able to remember times when an urge to drink passed even though they didn't drink. This can increase their confidence and understanding that an urge doesn't have to be acted upon. If the client expresses doubt, the therapist may ask *"Has there ever been a time when you had an urge to drink, but couldn't for some reason? What happened?"*

7. Talk it through

    Thoughts about drinking are common among people trying to quit drinking. Talking to helpful or supportive friends or family members can help you to understand some of the reasons you are having drinking thoughts. This understanding can help to manage troublesome drinking thoughts.

8. Distract yourself

    Finally, a way to cope with drinking thoughts may be to think about something that is completely unrelated to drinking. For example, directing your thoughts towards pleasant, enjoyable topics such as holiday plans, vacations spots, loved ones, a fond memory, or enjoyable hobbies can help to move away from drinking related thoughts.

Managing Emotions With Cognitive Reappraisal

In this section, you will demonstrate how reappraisal, or thinking differently about a situation, can impact your client's emotions. If the client can think differently about a situation, and prevent or reduce an unpleasant emotion, then the risk for drinking may be decreased. Sometimes, you may first have to work with your client to develop an awareness of how thoughts can impact behavior.

> *Thoughts constantly go through our minds. They happen very quickly and often we are unaware of them. Sometimes we act on our thoughts without stopping to evaluate if our actions are in line with our goals. We see this quite often in people who are beginning to change their drinking behavior. For example, many people are initially unaware of thoughts that precede the decision to drink. They often say "I don't think about drinking, I just drink" or "I just wanted a drink." In these instances, people may be acting without awareness of the reason(s) for wanting a drink. However, if we ask them why they want a drink, they often will say, "I'll feel better" or "I want to relax." In this case, the person may be feeling a certain level of stress or an unpleasant emotion and the immediate thought is "I want a drink." The person begins to think about the positive effects that a drink may bring. The decision occurs quickly and without much awareness or elaboration of the reasons why the person wants to drink. Cognitive Reappraisal involves taking time to observe and evaluate one's thoughts, providing an opportunity to think about the thought differently (reappraise) and choose a different path. In this example, a person might consider other alternative actions for managing their distress.*

What Is Cognitive Reappraisal?

Cognitive Reappraisal, in which an individual "thinks differently" about a situation or event, can be an effective strategy for managing emotions. It is a highly flexible strategy that can be used before, during, or after a stressful or distressing event. Ideally, if the client is able to anticipate an upcoming event, they can prepare by using Cognitive Reappraisal to enter the situation thinking differently about it. Once in the situation, they can remind themselves of this new way of thinking. Reappraisal can also be used effectively after the event when the client thinks, "Hey, that wasn't so bad."

In the emotion regulation literature, Cognitive Reappraisal is thought of as an *antecedent-focused* emotion regulation skill; it is most effective when applied *before* your client enters a negative emotion-related, high-risk drinking situation. It's a bit harder to apply the skill once the person has entered the high-risk situation and *after* the emotion has begun to develop and increase in intensity.

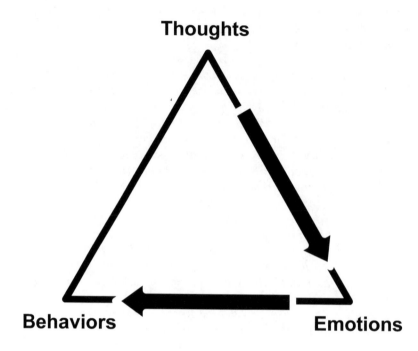

Figure 4 Relationship of Thought to Emotion and Behavior

When demonstrating Cognitive Reappraisal, look for situations in which your client's thoughts lead to unpleasant emotions. Ideally, you and your client should focus on a situation in which their thoughts and emotions are related to alcohol use. However, a nondrinking negative affect situation may also be used. It's more important to teach the skill in a situation that is personally relevant to your client than to use a less relevant situation that includes the use of alcohol. If your client can see the benefit of Cognitive Reappraisal in a nondrinking situation, they may be more likely to apply it at a later time to a negative emotional drinking situation.

You will review the relationship between thoughts, emotions, and behaviors (Figure 4) using a high-risk situation. Two examples are provided. Example 1 describes a situation in which the person can use reappraisal in advance of the high-risk situation. Example 2 demonstrates the use of Cognitive Reappraisal when the high-risk situation is more imminent.

Example 1: Family Event With Alcohol

Following a month of abstinence, this individual is obligated to attend her daughter's wedding, where alcohol will be served.

High-risk Situation →	Thoughts →	Emotions →	Possible Behaviors
- Daughter's wedding	- I'm going to have a hard time talking to people, no alcohol to help me loosen up and socialize. - Everyone's going to notice I'm not drinking . . . they'll think it's weird. - I feel like such a loser.	- Nervous, anxious - Embarrassed - Inadequate	- Skip the reception, think of excuses not to go. - Give up and have a drink just this once.

Example 2: Stressful Day at Work

After a stressful day at her job, where the supervisor assigned her a great deal of extra work, she is facing an evening at home when she would typically drink to manage her stress.

High-risk Situation →	Thoughts →	Emotions →	Possible Behaviors
- Difficult day—given extra work to do - Evening at home	- What a terrible day! - They don't know how much I have to do every day. - They don't appreciate me.	- Aggravated - Overwhelmed - Unappreciated	- Snap at people - Drag my heels - Be unproductive - Drink or have thoughts about drinking

Session 4: Thoughts, Urges, and Cravings

Implementing Cognitive Reappraisal Skills

> **TIP** Not all reappraisal prompts, noted next as questions, will be appropriate for every person or their specific situations. An effective Cognitive Reappraisal may not fit neatly into any one category; trying to generate reappraisals using only specific categories could unnecessarily limit a creative reappraisal process for some individuals. Other individuals may be better able to generate reappraisals after becoming familiar with the various types of reappraisals that demonstrate how people can think differently about their situations.

Reappraisal means looking at or thinking about your situation in a different way. It is an effective and useful strategy for helping people manage thoughts and emotions that may lead to drinking. Consider looking at your circumstances from a different angle by asking yourself:

General reappraisal prompt:

- *Is there another way to think about this situation?*

Specific reappraisal prompts:

- *How might others think about this situation? Stepping outside of ourselves to consider other perspectives or points of view can be an effective way to manage negative thoughts. If a friend or family member voiced these kinds of thoughts to you, what would you say to them?*
- *Are my thoughts and interpretations accurate? Just because we have a thought doesn't make it true. Ask yourself: Do these thoughts make sense? Are they logical? What is the evidence?*
- *What could I learn from this situation? If something doesn't turn out the way I wanted it to, what information can I gather so that future attempts are more likely to be successful?*
- *Might there be some positives here I haven't considered?*

"A Thought Is Just a Thought."

Thoughts are just that—thoughts. They may or may not be entirely accurate, or reflect our true opinions or values. Just because we have a thought doesn't make it true. *For example, we may believe that a coworker doesn't like us because she suddenly has become cool in her interactions with us. However, it also is possible that she is having difficulties in her own life that makes it tough for her to be friendly with people at work. How you think about this situation can also affect how you feel. You might feel hurt or angry if you interpreted her actions to mean that she didn't like you. Alternatively, you might feel empathy and compassion if you interpreted her actions as a sign that she may be struggling with some aspect of her personal life. Taking time to reappraise your coworker's behavior can reduce the intensity of your negative emotional reaction in this situation. Cognitive Reappraisal can be used at any time before, during, or after an event. Ideally, if you know of an upcoming event, you can prepare by using reappraisal beforehand and enter into the situation with a different way of thinking about it. Once in the situation, you can remind yourself of this new way of thinking. Reappraisal can also occur after the event, when you think to yourself, "Hey, that wasn't so bad."*

Reappraisal Examples

Example 1: Daughter's Wedding

Before Reappraisal

High-risk Situation →	**Thoughts** →	**Emotions** →	**Behavior**
- Daughter's wedding	- I'm going to have a hard time talking to people, no alcohol to help me loosen up and socialize. - Everyone's going to notice I'm not drinking ... they'll think it's weird. - I feel like such a loser.	- Nervous, anxious - Embarrassed - Inadequate	- Skip the reception, think of excuses not to go. - Give up and have a drink just this once.

After Reappraisal

High-risk Situation → **Thoughts** → **Emotions** → **Behavior**

- This is the first time doing this without alcohol. I'll never have to do it for the first time again.
- Some might notice, but they might be more curious than anything else.
- (For "I feel like such a loser")
- A thought is just a thought.

- Still nervous, but also a little hopeful (it'll get easier)
- Embarrassed, but not as much.
- Not inadequate ... maybe uncertain?

- Easier to abstain
- Think of ways to make myself feel more comfortable when I'm there.
- Make some specific plans to keep from drinking.

Example 2: Stressful Day at Work

Before Reappraisal

High-risk Situation → **Thoughts** → **Emotions** → **Behavior**

- Hard day—given extra work to do.
- Evening, at home.

- What a terrible day!
- They don't know how much I have to do every day.
- They don't appreciate me.

- Aggravated
- Overwhelmed
- Unappreciated

- Snap at people.
- Drag my heels
- Be unproductive ..
- Drink or have thoughts about drinking

After Reappraisal

High-risk Situation → **Thoughts** → **Emotions** → **Behavior**

- Well, it's over now and I got through it. I've had worse.
- Maybe they actually didn't realize how much I already had to do or how long it takes.
- Come to think of it, they did say how much they appreciated my help.

- A bit more confident (I can get through tough days)
- Not aggravated ... Maybe just annoyed.
- Pleased

- Easier to abstain
- Tell people I had a rough day.
- Decide to take it easy tonight, put my feet up.
- Have some good food.
- Go to bed earlier than usual.

In-Session Skill Practice: Cognitive Reappraisal

In this exercise, you and the client will work together to apply Cognitive Reappraisal to a negative emotional drinking situation that is salient for the client. Direct the client's attention to the first Managing Emotions: Thought Reappraisal worksheet provided in Chapter 6 of the client workbook. Have the client choose a personally relevant example (e.g., a frequent situation from the Daily Monitoring Log), and use the format provided to generate several Cognitive Reappraisals. Use the general prompt first (i.e., "Is there another way to look at this situation?"), then select one or two other specific reappraisal questions as needed. Write the reappraisals in the Thoughts column of the example. Adjust emotions and behavior according to the reappraisal. Discuss with your client the changes in emotion and behavior that would result from conducting a reappraisal of the situation. The therapist may also use other general reappraisal prompts such as *"Am I taking the whole picture into consideration? What else could be going on here?"*

At the end of the exercise, process this reappraisal exercise with the client. The purpose of this processing is to enhance the client's understanding that with Cognitive Reappraisal, emotions and behavior can change. Some sample questions and comments are:

> *What do you notice after you reappraised the situation?*
>
> *That's right, the emotion is different now. Just by looking at the situation differently, the emotions can change and the behaviors can change.*
>
> *So, by asking yourself "What else could be going on here?" you think differently about the situation. As you think differently about it, your feelings change and your risk for drinking is reduced. This relationship between thoughts, emotions, and behavior is something we have talked about.* (Show client a diagram of the thought–emotion–behavior triangle in Chapter 6 of client workbook, located in the Session Highlights). *We are coming at the behavior from both sides here, and it all started by considering if there was another way to think about it.*

TIP When using a positive reappraisal strategy, take care not to invalidate or minimize the client's difficulties. Positive reappraisal is not the same as "think positive" or "just focus on positive thoughts" and it is not to be equated with sayings that might seem trite like "When life gives you lemons, make lemonade." The purpose of positive reappraisal is to prompt the client to consider the bigger picture and acknowledge the actual or potential positive effects or benefits of whatever may be happening.

It is common for clients to make a statement indicating that they understand positive reappraisal to mean they should "think positive." When this occurs, a possible therapist response could be to initially agree (rather than correcting the client) and then add that it's about making sure positive aspects aren't left out of their thinking. For example *"Right, instead of just focusing on how sour the lemons are we can make lemonade. We still have sour lemons, but we also have lemonade."* It is important to convey to clients that reappraisal does not involve pushing unwanted thoughts away. We know that pushing away unwanted thoughts isn't effective for managing situations involving unpleasant emotions. We know that when people do this, the thoughts and emotions return. Reappraisal is different; it's about making sure our thoughts include alternative ways of looking at the situation, which can include the positive side of the story.

For the client's convenience, included in the workbook is a brief three-step guide that clients may use when applying the skill of Cognitive Reappraisal in everyday life. The three-step outline follows:

1. Breathe
2. Identify the thought
3. Reappraise

The client workbook also includes an extra example of how the client can apply reappraisal to managing thoughts about urges and cravings. For example, clients may think that their craving will grow stronger and become unbearable. A Cognitive Reappraisal of this thought might be, "I know that it will pass." Let your client know they are free to explore this and other examples using the Managing Urges and Cravings: Thought Reappraisal worksheet found in Chapter 6 of the companion workbook.

Between-Session Skill Practice

Work collaboratively with the client to mutually agree on a specific plan for between-session skill practice.

- Identify any drinking-related thoughts. Write them on the Daily Monitoring Log.
- Try out one or more of the coping skills for managing drinking-related thoughts.
- Add coping skills to the High-risk Situations and Coping Plan worksheet.
- Choose a Dedicated Mindfulness skill and practice for 3–5 minutes twice daily.

- Continue practicing Mindful Moments several times per day.
- Conduct a reappraisal for a negative emotional drinking situation using the Managing Emotions: Thought Reappraisal worksheet found in Chapter 6 of the companion workbook.

Making It Happen
- Build it into daily life.
- Think about when and where to rehearse skills.
- Use cues or prompts to remember to practice the skills.

Chapter 8

Session 5
Drink Refusal Skills and Managing Emotions With Actions

Materials

Managing Negative Emotions without Drinking workbook, Chapter 7

Therapist brief mindfulness exercise scripts, located in Chapters 5, 6, and 7 of this book

Session Overview

In this session, you will provide education regarding direct and indirect social pressure to drink and to teach drink refusal skills. This will include a role-play practice of an individualized high-risk situation. You will also review the relationship between thoughts, emotions, and behavior with an emphasis on the way in which changing a behavior can change how we feel. This often involves "acting the opposite of what an emotion is urging you to do." The client will be taught the five steps for managing emotions with actions and will work through a personalized high-risk drinking situation.

Session Outline

- Session introduction
- Drink refusal skills
- Managing emotions with actions
- Between-session skill practice

Session Introduction

Conduct Breathalyzer Test

Brief Mindfulness Exercise (3–5 Minutes)

The therapist may choose a brief mindfulness exercise of their own liking or offer the client the choice of any brief mindfulness exercises from Sessions 2–4.

Session 5: Drink Refusal and Emotions

Review Between-Session Skill Practice

Collaborate with the client to problem solve any barriers that may have interfered with skill practice. If the client is experiencing difficulties, see Chapter 3 of this guide for ways to increase client engagement with between-session skill practice.

Review Daily Monitoring Log

Over the course of treatment, you will have discussed a number of high-risk situations. Select several situations that are most relevant to the client at this point in treatment and probe for additional details including desire to drink or craving, skills, or strategies used, and the number of standard drinks consumed on each day. Provide reinforcement for past-week abstinence or progress toward abstinence.

Sample questions:

- *How have things been going?*
- *Over the past week, were there times when you wanted to drink?*
- *Let's look over the self-monitoring sheet . . . what were some ratings for your desire to drink?*
- *Is this a situation in which you tried to abstain? What did you do (skills or strategies) to get through it without drinking?*
- *How well did this work?*
- *What was your drinking like over the past week? How many standard drinks did you have on that day?*

Provide feedback on skills or strategies the client used to manage high-risk situations including both effective and ineffective strategies. If the client implemented ineffective strategies, collaborate with the client to generate alternative strategies that could be more effective. Discuss upcoming high-risk situations that may pose a unique challenge to abstinence or require additional attention.

Drink Refusal Skills

Rationale and Information

Drink refusal skills address two forms of social or peer pressure that are often experienced by individuals in recovery: direct and indirect social pressure. Direct social pressure occurs when someone directly offers the individual a drink, while indirect pressure occurs when someone with an alcohol problem returns to the same old settings (e.g., bars, get-togethers, parties), with the same people, doing the same things, and experiences feelings previously associated with drinking. What follows are some options for an assertive response to an invitation to drink. At the outset, some clients will state that drink refusal skills are not necessary because they only drink when alone. For these clients, please refer to the box entitled "A Different Path" that appears later in this chapter.

Social pressure to drink can take two forms:

1. **Direct social pressure:** *when someone offers you a drink or the opportunity to drink*
2. **Indirect social pressure:** *when you feel tempted to drink just by being around others who are drinking, even though you are not being offered a drink, for example, a summer family picnic where others are drinking. While you may not have a drink at the picnic, watching many people drinking around you can trigger thoughts about returning home and having a drink.*

Take a moment to think about some situations where you experience either direct or indirect social pressure to drink.

Although it's helpful to avoid people, places, and things that involve drinking such as bars, everybody is going to run into situations where there will be some pressure to drink. Being offered or pressured to drink is a high-risk situation for many individuals who have decided to stop drinking. Being able to turn down an offer of a drink is an assertiveness skill that often requires conscious effort until a person reaches a point where it occurs automatically. Let's talk about what it's like to be pressured to drink and then move on to talking about how to refuse drinks assertively.

- *Have you received such offers or experienced this type of pressure?*
- *Do you have someone in your life that pressures you to drink?*
- *What is that like for you?*

It is important to provide the client with a rationale for practicing drink refusal that covers the following points:

1. The risk for relapse is higher without effective coping skills.
2. Drink refusal takes a specific type of assertiveness skill that goes beyond just a sincere desire to stop.
3. The social use of alcohol is very common.
4. Practicing the skill increases its effectiveness including the speed and efficiency of the response.

Provide the client with the following directions and information regarding how to go about refusing a drink:

How you choose to respond to an invitation to drink will vary, depending on who is offering the drink and how the offer is made. Sometimes a simple "No, thank you" will be enough.

At other times, additional strategies may be necessary. In some cases, telling the other person about your prior drinking problem will be useful in eliciting helpful support; at other times, it will be unnecessary to share this information.

The more quickly and confidently you say "no" to offers of a drink, the less likely this type of situation will result in a lapse or relapse. In this case, action leads to success. Why? Well, the old saying "He who hesitates is lost" offers us an answer. If your behavior suggests to the other person that you are unsure or hesitant, this can allow the person offering the drink a second opportunity to "twist your arm." In addition, in that moment of hesitation, you might think, "One beer wouldn't be so bad." The goal then is to take action and learn to say "no" in a quick and convincing manner and to have your response at the tip of your tongue. Today, we will talk about some new skills or tools for your toolbox called drink refusal skills.

Drink Refusal Skills

Review these skills with the client, answering questions and providing clarification, as needed:

- Tip: Get a nonalcoholic drink immediately or bring one with you.
- Plan an exit strategy *before* you enter the situation.
- Say "no" first.
- Suggest something else to eat, drink, or do:

    "No thanks. Would you like to take a walk instead?"
    "No thanks, but I'd sure like a cup of coffee."

- Ask the person to stop offering you a drink.

    "No thanks, no need to keep offering. I'll let you know if I change my mind."

- After saying "no," change the subject.
- Use your body language:

    Use a clear, firm, unhesitating voice.
    Make direct eye contact.

- There's no need to make excuses or feel guilty: You have the right *not* to drink!

Drink Refusal Role Play

Practice is an important aspect of skill acquisition. Allow time to practice the new skills in session. Begin by inquiring about specific high-risk situations in which the client feels pressured to drink. This allows the client to practice situations that are personally relevant:

- *Tell me about a specific situation where someone frequently or strongly pressured you to drink?*
- *Where were you? What did the person say? How did they say it?*
- *What is it about this situation that made it most difficult to say "no"?*
- *What might you have said or done differently?*

> *Now that you have told me what you might say or do in this situation, I think it would be valuable if we role played this situation. This would help me to gain a better understanding of the situation and can give you an opportunity to try out this new way to manage it. If it's all right with you, I'll play the part of the person who is offering you the drink, and you can play yourself.*

This initial role play provides you with an opportunity to assess the client's drink refusal skills, paying attention to the client's verbal and nonverbal (e.g., eye contact, posture) behavior.

Following the role play, engage the client in a discussion of the role play and offer constructive feedback:

- *Great! What was that like for you?*
- *What do you think you did well?*
- *What do you think you could improve on next time?*
- *Are there any situations coming up where you anticipate being pressured to drink?*

If time permits, repeat the role play. At times, it may be helpful for you to play the role of the client in order to model a new drink refusal skill or a skill variant that the client is having difficulty executing. The purpose of the in-session role play is to train a new behavioral response and to facilitate responding in "real world" situations.

 A Different Path

Clients who report drinking only when they are alone may not see the relevance of drink refusal skills. If this is the case, more time should be spent discussing indirect social pressure situations. Alternatively, you may acknowledge that such skills may not seem relevant now, but that they could be useful in the future. You can relate the following case example:

> *Joe only drank at home alone in the evenings. At social gatherings, he reported no problems saying "no" when offered a drink. At such times, he would think to himself, "I'll have a drink when I get home." He was usually the first one to leave these social events because of his desire to return home and drink. People would comment on his early departure and would ask him to stay. He would always refuse. As he entered treatment and became abstinent, he began to find it more difficult to say "no" when offered a drink socially. He no longer kept alcohol in the house and knew that drinking at home alone was no longer an option. The therapist worked with Joe to implement drink refusal skills when offered a drink in these situations and also worked with him to develop a plan for managing his urges and cravings once he returned home and was alone. The plan involved having a favorite nonalcoholic beverage and snack waiting for him at home.*

Managing Emotions With Actions

Rationale and Information

By definition, emotions are associated with urges to act in particular ways. Fear creates the urge to escape, sadness creates the urge to withdraw, and anger creates the urge to fight. Of course, people do not always act out these urges. Although these actions may have had adaptive value for our ancestors, in today's world some urges to act may be ineffective, unhealthy, and even harmful to one's best interest (e.g., a fight with one's boss resulting in a loss of job). One way to manage emotions is to take a different action, or to substitute an adaptive behavior for a maladaptive behavior. In this ERT session, you will introduce the idea that actions can lead to changes in emotions. You will use the CBT Triangle model to illustrate the path between behavior and emotion and teach your client a series of five steps for managing emotion with actions.

Provide a refresher for the client on the CBT model and the function or purpose of emotions (covered in earlier treatment sessions, particularly Session 1). Be sure the client understands how behavioral urges fit within this model so that they also understand how this session's skills will help

Session 5: Drink Refusal and Emotions

them with their goals of adaptively managing emotions and substituting healthier coping behaviors for drinking.

We know that thoughts, emotions, and behaviors can influence one another, and that we can intervene at any point on this "triangle" (Figure 5) to bring about a change. The focus of this treatment is on your emotions and how managing unpleasant emotions can help you to manage your drinking behavior. That is, you are more likely to achieve and maintain abstinence if you have alternative skills for managing uncomfortable emotions. Today, we will take a closer look at how you can use actions or behaviors to modify or change your emotions. Through your actions, you can bring about a change in how you feel. And again, if you can better regulate your unpleasant emotions, then you decrease the likelihood of drinking to cope with those feelings.

You may remember that emotions serve an important function. Uncomfortable emotions give us valuable information; they grab our attention and let us know that something is wrong. The emotion provides us with the drive or motivation to take action. This drive to take action is described as an urge to act. An urge is the feeling that happens right before a behavior occurs. For people with an alcohol problem, an unpleasant emotion may trigger the urge to drink. In this example, drinking is the action the person takes to manage the unpleasant emotion. But how do you manage the unpleasant emotion when you are no longer drinking? What action can you take to help you manage the emotion?

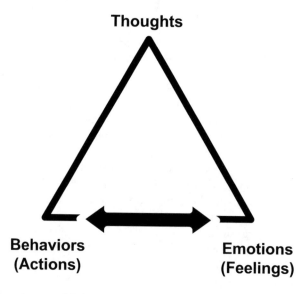

Figure 5 Emotions and Behaviors Affect One Another

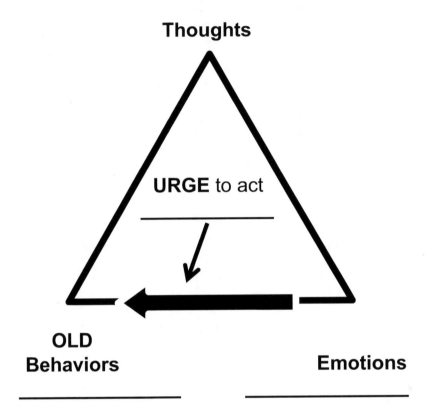

Figure 6 Emotion Produced an Urge to Act

A common strategy involves "acting the opposite," to what the emotion is "urging" you do (Barlow et al., 2004; Linehan, 1993, 2015). This works well when the action you feel like taking is either harmful or ineffective, or when the emotion doesn't fit the facts of the situation. In the first case, yelling at your boss because you are angry about being asked to work overtime may be harmful to your chances of promotion to supervisor or even keeping your job, and therefore is not effective. In this case, acting opposite would involve taking three deep breaths and avoiding a direct confrontation. It may be the case that your contract specified that you might be asked to work overtime and you were given one week's notice of the overtime. In this case, your level of anger may not be justified, or may not fit the facts of the situation. Again, in this case, acting opposite to your initial urge to yell at your boss is likely the more effective and adaptive action to take. This may involve some planning and effort on your part, but with practice, you can successfully change your behavior. An important point to remember is that you are selecting a behavior to help you cope with or manage an unpleasant emotion. Your primary goal is to choose a behavior that is effective, healthy, and adaptive.

To facilitate the client's understanding of this strategy, ask the client to identify a recent situation in which they experienced an emotion-driven urge to act in a particular way, but then decided to do something different. Identify the emotion in this situation, the action the emotion was provoking, and the alternative action they took. Use the following questions to guide your discussion:

- *What emotion did you experience?*
- *What action was the emotion leading you to take?*
- *How would you describe the initial urge to act? Was it a thought, a physical sensation?*
- *What happened that helped you to decide on a different course of action?*
- *What alternative action did you take?*
- *Was the alternative action (or lack of action) helpful, healthy, or beneficial to you?*

In-Session Skill Practice: Managing Emotions With Actions

In the situation you just described, you chose to act in a way that was different from the urge you felt. Let's take a look at one of your situations in which you are at risk for drinking due to uncomfortable emotions using the behavior and emotion part of the triangle.

Next, have the client identify a negative emotional drinking situation. Review the following steps for managing emotions with actions and assist the client in completing the In-Session Skill Practice: Managing Emotions With Actions worksheet. This will orient the client to the general process of managing emotions with actions.

Steps For Managing Emotions With Actions

1. Stop and Notice

- *Use this mindfulness skill to increase awareness of unpleasant emotions and urges to act. Cue or prompt yourself to "Stop and Notice" several times each day by setting an alarm on your phone or posting a note that you see throughout the day.*

2. Identify the Emotion

- *If necessary, use the Emotions List from Chapter 3 of your workbook.*
- *Use your thoughts and physical sensations to guide you.*
- *Ask yourself if this is an emotion that you want to change.*

3. Evaluate the Urge to Act

- *What does this emotion make me feel like doing?*
- *Is this a good idea?*
- *Is it helpful?*
- *Is it healthy?*
- *Will it help me achieve my goals? Will it keep me safe? Will it keep me sober?*

   If the specific action would be helpful or a good idea for the situation at hand and fits with your overall goals of a healthy behavior that avoids drinking, then give yourself the "go-ahead" to take action. However, if the specific action would not be healthy, helpful, or does not fit with your overall goals of health and abstinence, then choose an alternative action. This is a way of behaving or "acting" yourself into feeling differently.

4. Choose an Alternative Action

- *A common guideline is to consider actions that are in some way opposite or inconsistent with your initial urge to act.*
- *Remind yourself of your goal, which is to regulate or change the emotion.*
- *You can ask yourself "What healthy or effective action will help me achieve my goal?"*
- *Let's brainstorm some ideas.*
- *What is the first step? The second step?*

5. Take Action

- *Take a deep breath and take action!*
- *Re-evaluate your emotion.*
- *Give yourself a big pat on the back for facing a challenging situation.*

Between-Session Skill Practice

- Identify a Dedicated Mindfulness exercise of choice to practice for 3–5 minutes, two or three times/day.
- Practice Mindful Moments five times per day.
- Continue Daily Monitoring Log.
- Complete drink refusal skill practice.
- Manage an emotion with action, completing Between-Session Skill Practice Worksheet: Managing Emotions With Actions.

Making It Happen

- Build it into daily life.
- Think about when and where to rehearse skills.
- Use reminders or cues to practice the skills.

Chapter 9

Session 6

Skill and Treatment Progress Review and Preparing for Direct Experiencing of Emotion

Materials

Managing Negative Emotions Without Drinking workbook, Chapter 8

Therapist brief mindfulness exercise scripts, located in Chapters 5, 6, and 7 of this book

Therapist Form: Scene Development worksheet (Appendix B)

Session Overview

In this session you will review coping skills learned thus far and the client's progress towards their drinking goals. You will work with the client to prepare them for the direct experiencing of emotion sessions. This will include the guided imagery lemon exercise and the gathering of information for the first direct experiencing scene using the Scene Development worksheet provided in this guide's Appendix B.

> ✎ Note: As a complement to the material in this session, the client workbook contains additional information regarding problem-solving skills that are not addressed in this session. This includes a problem-solving exercise that demonstrates how a number of skills can be used to manage a high-risk drinking situation involving an unpleasant emotion. This exercise provides the client with an opportunity to apply the problem-solving method to a personalized negative-affect drinking situation.

Session Outline

- Session introduction
- Review treatment goals
- Review coping skills
- Rationale for direct experiencing of emotion
- Guided imagery lemon exercise
- Scene development
- Between-session skill practice

Session Introduction

Conduct Breathalyzer Test

Brief Mindfulness Exercise (3–5 Minutes)

Begin the session with a brief mindfulness exercise. You can choose an exercise or offer the client choice of any brief mindfulness exercises from Sessions 2–4.

Review Between-Session Skill Practice

Continue to be diligent about exploring difficulties the client may be experiencing with between-session skill practice. Although some clients may consistently be practicing new skills, others may be having difficulties fitting skill practice into each day. Research continues to demonstrate a strong link between engaging in between-session practice and positive treatment outcomes. If the client is experiencing difficulties, see Chapter 3 of this guide for ways to increase client engagement with between-session skill practice.

Reinforce Successful Skill Use and Progress

In addition to reinforcing the client's practice of skills taught in the previous session, reinforce the client's use of any other skills he has used over the prior week. Additionally, provide reinforcement for past week abstinence or for progress towards the goal of abstinence.

Sample questions:

- Are any high-risk situations becoming easier to manage?
- Were there times over the past week when you wanted to drink, but didn't?

Review Daily Monitoring Log

Engage the client in a discussion of the type of high-risk situations encountered over the past week, intensity of desire to drink or craving in these situations, and the skills or strategies the client used or attempted to use to manage these high-risk situations. If they consumed alcohol, review the amount of alcohol consumed daily using standard drink sizes.

Sample questions:

- *How have things been going?*
- *Over the past week, were there times when you wanted to drink?*
- *Let's look over the monitoring sheet . . . what were some ratings for your desire to drink?*
- *Is this a situation in which you tried to abstain? What did you do (skills or strategies) to get through it without drinking?*
- *How well did this work?*
- *What was your drinking like over the past week?*
- *How many standard drinks did you have on that day?*

Provide feedback on the skills or strategies the client used during the past week, including the effectiveness of the skills. This includes suggesting a different skill or set of skills that the client can use in the situation. This is particularly important for more difficult high-risk situations that may pose a unique challenge to the client, or that require additional attention. Enquire about any upcoming high-risk situations that may be used for an upcoming discussion of high-risk situations later in this session.

Review Treatment Goals and Progress

Briefly review the client's progress towards their drinking goals. Have their drinking goals changed since the beginning of treatment? If so, how? For example, it is not uncommon for clients who began treatment feeling ambivalent regarding a drinking goal of lifelong abstinence to become more certain over time that they would like to be abstinent for life. Following this review of the drinking goals, transition to reviewing the skills discussed in the previous session.

> *This is the midpoint of the treatment program and I would like to check in with you regarding your goals and progress toward those goals. After that, we will take some time and review the skills that we've covered in our previous meetings.*
>
> *When you entered treatment, your goal was to _____ (be abstinent or reduce your drinking). What are your thoughts about this now?*
>
> *How would you rate your progress towards achieving this goal?*
>
> *What do you think would help you continue (or maintain) your progress?*

You're right where you want to be. Good! Today we're going to review the skills we've discussed thus far. This presents on opportunity to reflect on what has been working for you.

 A Different Path

If the client is progressing more gradually than expected:

You've made progress, but you still have some work to do before meeting your goal. What do you think would help you reach your goal?

In addition, it may be helpful at this point to clarify the client's goals and expectations for progress at this midpoint in treatment. What progress has been made so far? What was instrumental in bringing about that progress? What might be getting in the way of further progress?

Skills Review

This week presents an opportunity for us to review the skills we've covered thus far. It may be a good time to take a closer look at these skills and see which ones could be helpful to you moving forward.

Review the skills that have been taught from the beginning of the treatment program, encouraging questions and comments from the client. The client should be encouraged to try out different skills, whenever the opportunity presents itself. The client should also be directed to Chapter 8 of the workbook, where the client will find additional materials on problem solving including problem-solving steps and a list of coping skills.

Discuss when certain skills might be most helpful, but also acknowledge that flexible use of the skills is important to effective emotion regulation. That is, if one skill doesn't seem to be working in a given situation, try a different skill. Remind clients that some exercises can be practiced most anytime, anywhere. Other skills may be used to prepare for upcoming high-risk situations including Cognitive Reappraisal or drink refusal skills. Other skills are useful in the moment, and can be used when the client is actually experiencing a craving or emotional response. Skills that may be used in these different situations include:

- Mindful Observing
- Stop and Notice
- Body Scan
- Object-centered mindfulness
- Self-monitoring
- Watch the Wave (for emotions and urges)
- Other coping skills for managing urges and cravings (i.e., avoid people or situations, decision delay, food or nonalcoholic drink, talk to a friend, distraction)
- Mindful Breathing
- Cognitive Reappraisal
- Drink refusal skills
- Managing emotions with actions

Preparing for Direct Experiencing of Emotion: Increasing Motivation to Engage With Negative Affect

Prior to moving forward with this session, it is important that you read Chapter 3 of this guide, which provides important information and guidelines for conducting the direct experiencing of emotion sessions.

There are a number of strategies you can use to increase the likelihood the client will engage in imaginal exposure to high-risk drinking situations involving unpleasant emotions conducted in Sessions 7–10. Up to this point in the treatment, the importance of directly facing uncomfortable emotions, the rationale for the exposure scenes, and the skills needed to successfully navigate these scenes have been woven throughout previous sessions. Mindfulness skills (in particular, Mindful Observing) and "watching the wave" direct the client to engage with their present experience including emotional discomfort and craving. Being able to engage with one's emotions in the present moment is important preparation for the direct experiencing of emotion sessions.

As a way to introduce the client to the direct experiencing of emotion, the more familiar concept of "imagery" is used with the client. The analogy to watching a movie is introduced to the client and is developed further in subsequent sessions. This movie analogy is helpful in explaining to clients the concept of "moving" to specific locations within their negative-affect drinking scene—both "fast forward" and "rewind." An emotion-neutral exercise is conducted to provide an opportunity for the client to have a positive introductory imagery experience, increase the client's comfort in using imaginal techniques, and demonstrate the effectiveness of visual imagery as a method for exploring their negative-affect drinking situations.

> In previous sessions, we talked about mindfulness and how it can be used to increase our awareness of the present moment. By strengthening your attention to the present, you can become more aware of thoughts, feelings, and physical sensations when you find yourself in a high-risk drinking situation. In the next part of today's session, we will begin to merge the mindfulness skills that you are learning with guided imagery. Imagery involves having you imagine a situation that is familiar to you, that is, an actual situation that has happened in the past. Think of it as similar to scenes from a movie. As you imagine the scene, it becomes vivid and real, as if you are really there. We'll be using these imagery techniques to help you practice managing the emotions that are related to your drinking.
>
> I'd like to start by demonstrating the imagery technique. I usually begin with something that most people find easy to imagine—slicing a lemon. Is it okay if we do that?

Guided Imagery Lemon Exercise

This imagery scene should be read at a somewhat slower pace in order to allow the client time to imagine the details you are describing.

> Imagine yourself standing in your kitchen. Make this image as vivid as you can . . . imagine yourself as if you were there right now. Now imagine that you have a beautiful ripe lemon on the cutting board in front of you. Notice the bright yellow color. Pick the lemon up and feel the bumpy texture of the skin. Give it a little squeeze to feel that it is perfectly ripe. Now imagine putting the lemon back down on the cutting board. Pick up the knife and cut the lemon in half. As you cut, notice the beads of lemon juice rolling down on to the cutting board. You can immediately smell the strong lemon scent. Now cut a small slice of the lemon. Pick up this juicy slice of lemon and imagine taking a nice big bite of it.

Now ask the client to open their eyes.

> If you are like most people, you probably noticed a puckering in your mouth. This is an example of how powerful your imagination can be . . . with a simple imagery exercise, you reacted as if the image was real! What was this experience like for you?
>
> In the next several sessions, we'll use something like the lemon exercise to improve your ability to manage high-risk drinking situations,

especially those involving uncomfortable emotions that are related to drinking. Instead of the lemon, we'll slow things down and go through your high-risk drinking situation step-by-step, so you can get through them without drinking while managing your emotions in a healthier, more effective way. We'll pay attention to the same kind of valuable information that is listed on your monitoring log sheets such as thoughts, emotions, urges, cravings, and so on.

Direct Experiencing of Emotion Scene Development

Let's take a few minutes and talk about situations involving unpleasant thoughts, emotions, or physical sensations that increase your risk for drinking.

Using the Scene Development worksheet (Appendix B), gather information for the first exposure scene. This will include details of the high-risk situation such as who is present, and the client's thoughts and emotions associated with this situation. Importantly, it will also include urges and cravings for alcohol. This information gathering should take about 3–5 minutes. If the client is unsure about how to answer some of the questions, you can move on, making a note to see if the information can be gathered during the first exposure scene.

 A Different Path

What if the Client States Drinking is Unrelated to Negative Affect?

Some people may insist they do not experience negative emotions or cravings before drinking. Often, they will say something like "I just drink; I don't think about it" or "It just happens; I'm not feeling anything before I drink." Although it is preferable that the client identify a negative emotional drinking situation, it is not absolutely necessary for them to do so in order for the client to benefit from this approach. If the client is unable to identify such a situation, ask about the client's typical or usual drinking situations or a situation that occurs on most drinking days. It also could be a specific time of day that frequently is associated with drinking. Alternatively, identify a situation in which the client might find it difficult to abstain from drinking. It is likely that once the imagery scene is presented to the client, they will be able to more clearly articulate unpleasant emotions associated with the high-risk drinking situation.

We now have a high-risk drinking situation for the direct experiencing of emotion guided imagery scene. We will stop here for today and pick up from here next session. Do you have any questions before we end today?

Between-Session Skill Practice

- Identify a Dedicated Mindfulness exercise of choice to practice for 3–5 minutes, two or three times per day.
- Practice Mindful Moments, five times per day.
- Complete the Daily Monitoring Log.
- Continue with skill practice, daily if possible.
- The client may work on optional problem-solving material in Chapter 8 of the client workbook.

Making It Happen

- Build it into daily life.
- Think about when and where to rehearse skills.
- Use reminders or cues to practice the skills.

Chapter 10

Session 7
Coping With a Lapse or Relapse and Direct Experiencing of Emotion

Materials

Managing Negative Emotions Without Drinking workbook, Chapter 9
Managing Negative Emotions Without Drinking workbook, Chapter 8: Menu of Coping Skills and Strategies
Therapist brief mindfulness exercise scripts, located in Chapters 5, 6, and 7 of this book
Therapist form: Individual Distress Scale (Appendix C)
Therapist form: Direct Experiencing of Emotion recording form (Appendix D)

Session Goals

In this session, clients will continue to identify personalized high-risk drinking situations including those with both positive and negative affect. In addition to situations that occur frequently, the client will be asked to consider high-risk situations that occur less frequently but pose a significant risk for drinking. Coping plans to prevent drinking in these different types of situations will be developed. The rationale for the direct experience of emotion is provided and the client is informed that the presentation of these imagery scenes will take place over the next several sessions. Finally, distress and craving rating scales are reviewed and an initial negative emotional drinking scene is presented, including post-scene processing with the client.

Session Outline

- Session introduction
- Coping with a lapse or relapse
- Back on track: what to do if a lapse or relapse occurs
- Introduction to the direct experiencing of emotion
- Between-session skill practice

Session Introduction

Conduct Breathalyzer Test

Brief Mindfulness Exercise (3–5 Minutes)

Choose a brief mindfulness exercise or offer the client the choice of any brief mindfulness exercises from Sessions 2–4.

Review Between-Session Skill Practice

Collaborate with the client to problem solve any barriers that may have interfered with skill rehearsal since the last treatment session. At this point in the treatment, some clients will have little difficulty with between-session skill practice, while others may still be experiencing difficulties completing practice regularly. If the client continues to experience difficulties, see Chapter 3 of this guide for ways to increase client engagement with between-session skill practice.

Reinforce Successful Skill Use and Progress

This can be accomplished while reviewing the Daily Monitoring Log, if desired. Reinforce the client's use of skills used over the past week. In addition, provide verbal reinforcement for abstinence over the past week or for progress towards abstinence.

Sample questions:

- *Are any high-risk situations becoming easier to manage?*
- *Were there times over the past week when you wanted to drink, but didn't?*

Review Daily Monitoring Log

Engage the client in a discussion of the type of high-risk situations they have encountered since the last session, the intensity of desire to drink or craving in these situations, and the skills or strategies they used to manage these high-risk situations. If they consumed alcohol, review the amount of alcohol consumed daily using standard drink sizes.

Sample questions:

- *How have things been going?*
- *Over the past week, were there times when you wanted to drink?*
- *Let's look over the monitoring sheet . . . what were some ratings for your desire to drink?*
- *Is this a situation in which you tried to abstain?*

- *What did you do* (skills or strategies) *to get through it without drinking?*
- *How well did this work?*
- *What was your drinking like over the past week?*
- *How many standard drinks did you have on that day?*

Provide feedback on the skills or strategies that the client used since the last session including the effectiveness of the skills. This may include suggesting a different skill or set of skills that the client can use in the situation. This is particularly important for more difficult high-risk situations that may pose a unique challenge to the client, or that require additional attention. Inquire about any upcoming events that may be used for discussion of high-risk situations later in this session.

Preventing and Coping With a Relapse

Introduction

You have worked with the client in previous sessions to identify his usual or frequent high-risk situations. Building on this work, develop a list with the client of potentially important high-risk situations they may face in the future. These often fall into the following categories: (1) major life transitions, (2) celebratory occasions, (3) unpleasant emotional situations (e.g., problems with a supervisor, visit from a difficult relative), (4) loss of important social relationships (e.g., divorce, death of spouse), and (5) other unexpected or major life events (e.g., health problems, job loss). Work with the client to formulate a plan to address these situations, should they occur. This presents a good opportunity to review the client's general plan for coping with high-risk situations, including drafting a list of potential social supports. Develop plans in the event that the client experiences a lapse or relapse to alcohol use. The goal for such a plan is to provide steps so that the client is prepared to get back to their sober lifestyle as soon as possible. Such a plan should highlight the importance of avoiding thinking of themselves as a failure, as lacking willpower, or any kind of thinking that might prolong the drinking behavior. Education about the relapse *process* and how to manage a lapse or relapse should it occur may better equip clients to navigate the sometimes difficult process of attaining abstinence.

> *So far, we have focused on your usual or more frequent high-risk situations and how to cope with them without drinking. Today we are going to give some thought to high-risk situations that may occur unexpectedly or that may occur less frequently, but are still important. These can include a variety of different situations. We'll begin preparing a coping plan for those specific situations. Then we will*

> *review a more general coping plan that can be used when you find yourself in any type of high-risk situation. Although planning ahead and practicing the plan will go a long way toward preventing drinking from happening, it's not uncommon for people to "slip" and drink. We will take some time to talk about what to do in case that happens.*

Major Life Events That May Increase the Risk for Drinking

> *Major life events and changes can be disruptive to your ongoing sobriety and can increase the risk for drinking. Such unexpected or infrequent events might include relationship changes or losses such as a break-up, a friend or family member moving away, a change in health for you or someone close to you, new responsibilities, work-related changes or events, or financial changes. Life events do not necessarily have to be negative to trigger a relapse. Life changes, even if positive, can also pose a risk, for example, a new relationship, receiving a promotion, a graduation, wedding, or even something as simple as a wide-open sunny day with no responsibilities that leaves you feeling content and wanting to extend that positive feeling by having a drink.*

- *What other events or situations might you add to this list?*
- *What other situations can you add to your high-risk situations, having thought about it in this new way?*

The client may write these identified life events or situations in their Personal Coping Plan in the workbook, Chapter 9, now or at a later time.

> *Let's take a look at the Menu of Coping Strategies and Skills from the last session and see which coping skills might work best for you in the high-risk situations we just identified.*

Encourage the client to write down several coping strategies for at least one of their newly identified high-risk situations. Certain coping skills may be particularly well-suited to a specific high-risk situation, while other coping skills may apply more generally to a number of different situations. The client may already be implementing some of these coping skills for previously identified high-risk situations. If the client is already using particular coping skills in multiple high-risk situations, this may identify skills that are especially beneficial to this particular client. Often, this indicates that the client is able to demonstrate flexible use of coping skills. If, on the other hand, it seems that the client is relying too heavily on a limited number of skills, provide encouragement to expand their repertoire of coping behaviors.

> We have talked about coping plans for very specific high-risk situations. Next, I'd like to work together on a more general coping plan that can be used when you find yourself in virtually any type of high-risk drinking situation. These coping skills can help you get through such times by providing you with alternatives to drinking.

Together with the client, review and discuss "If I encounter a high-risk situation" in their Personal Coping Plan. This is an opportunity for the client to add some specific strategies to this list.

> One of the most helpful things you can do is to first stop and take a breath. Then bring yourself to the present moment. In fact, in most guidelines to problem solving or decision making this is the first step. It makes sense if you think about it. Stopping and taking a breath allows you to give your situation some thought and choose how you would like to respond in this situation. Instead of an automatic, knee-jerk reaction, you can find healthier, more adaptive ways to respond to the situation.
>
> Another way to cope with difficult or high-risk situations is to make a connection to a supportive person. Is there someone who could provide this support to you?

Encourage the client to write down the names and numbers of several people who could provide support. This activity should be limited in scope as social support will be the focus of the next session. The client may write some or all of these names on their Personal Coping Plan.

 A Different Path

Client is reluctant to discuss the possibility of major life events, a lapse, or a relapse.

Regarding unexpected, infrequent, or unusual high-risk situations, the therapist may remind the client of the effectiveness of developing a coping plan in advance of encountering a high-risk situation:

> In previous sessions, we have focused on coping with situations in which you experience thoughts, cravings, and urges to drink.

Session 7: Coping With a Relapse

> *If you take time now to formulate a plan for how to cope with these frequently occurring situations, then you are more likely to get through them without drinking. Events and situations that don't occur as often, but that still pose a significant risk for drinking, also require some thought. Developing a plan for unexpected, infrequent, or unusual high-risk situations is very important as well, especially for preventing a lapse or relapse.*

In addition to providing a rationale for developing a relapse prevention plan, explore reasons for the client's reluctance to discuss these situations. In many cases, clients may not want to discuss these topics because they are avoiding uncomfortable emotions. Any opportunity for you to reinforce the importance and value of engaging with emotional discomfort is a good one. In this case, the discomfort serves to motivate clients to put effort into planning ahead in case this event occurs. The fire drill analogy, described next, also may be helpful.

Another common reason for reluctance is that clients have been successful in abstaining or significantly reducing their alcohol consumption and may not understand the importance of continuing to prepare for high-risk situations. The following rationale may be helpful when this is the case:

> *It's easy to get lulled into a false sense of security, especially when problems related to drinking seem to have faded into the past. In alcohol treatment, the first priority is to stop the problem use of alcohol. Next, the priority shifts to preventing the alcohol problem from returning. Often, people don't like to think or talk about this topic, especially when the problem seems to be getting better. However, in talking to many others who have had similar problems with alcohol, we have found that it is helpful to address this area in order to protect your ongoing sobriety.*

Fire drill analogy: The example of a fire drill can be used for both instances described earlier, that is, when a client is avoiding uncomfortable emotions and when a client has achieved a period of abstinence or significantly reduced alcohol consumption. Whether the "fire" is a difficult life event or a relapse, this analogy can demonstrate the value of planning for an event that, however unlikely, could have unwelcome or potentially serious consequences. The analogy of a "small fire" can illustrate the value of being able to quickly recognize advance warning signs (if present) and begin taking steps to address the problem, before the small fire becomes a much larger fire. A small fire can be likened to a lapse that if quickly addressed, can prevent a full-blown relapse:

> *It can be helpful to view this as similar to a fire drill. We hope that a fire never happens, but if it does, it is important to know what to do. For a drill to be effective, the actions must be rehearsed so that they can be easily remembered when the time comes for action. If a small fire does start, often it can be quickly extinguished if the person knows what to do and has the resources at hand, like a fire extinguisher. Any damage that might have occurred as a result of the fire is either avoided or minimized. In the same way, if someone "slips" and drinks, the right coping response can prevent or stop the drinking early enough to prevent a full-blown relapse. We'll take some time today to talk about some effective coping strategies for avoiding or reducing the impact of a slip.*

Back on Track: What to Do if a Relapse Occurs

> *High-risk situations increase the likelihood of drinking. Sometimes even with our best efforts, a return to drinking may occur. This is sometimes referred to as a "slip." A return to drinking is not unusual when it comes to making this kind of significant behavior change. Sometimes the slip is brief—we refer to this as a lapse. If drinking continues, perhaps returning to previous problematic levels, we refer to this as a relapse. In either case, how a person handles a lapse or a relapse can make a big difference in how quickly the person is able to get back to being abstinent. It's important not to allow a lapse or relapse to lead to thinking such as "I blew it" or "Now I have to start all over again." Instead, it is truly an opportunity to learn how it happened so that you can adapt your coping plans accordingly.*

Review the strategies for what to do in the event of a relapse allowing for a brief discussion of information the client finds unclear (see the Getting Back on Track information sheet in Chapter 9 of the client workbook).

The following steps can be helpful in the event of a relapse:

1. **Get rid of the alcohol and/or leave the place where the drinking occurred.** Remember that control is only a moment away.

2. **Stop the lapse from becoming a relapse.** See the lapse as a specific event rather than a "sign" that you can't have a sober lifestyle or that treatment isn't working. A drinking episode can't take away all that you have learned or your successes.
3. **Make immediate plans for getting yourself back on track.**
4. **Get in touch with people who help you stay sober.** This can be a friend, family member, or anyone else who supports your sobriety.
5. **Be open to examining how and why the relapse occurred.** This can help to reduce the amount of guilt or shame you may feel as those thoughts can lead to a feeling of hopelessness and continued drinking.
6. **Remember that a relapse is a learning experience that can help you maintain your sobriety in the long run.** Analyze the triggers for the lapse. Some usual triggers are anger, frustration, stress, celebrations, alcohol cues, and testing your own personal control.
7. **Discuss the relapse with your therapist.** Together you can make a plan for lasting sobriety. If you're not in treatment at the time, seek out help if necessary.
8. **Examine your expectations about drinking at the time of the relapse.** That is, what did you expect or hope that drinking would do for you?
9. **Renew your commitment to abstinence.**
10. **Make a plan for dealing with any consequences of the relapse.**

Introduction to Direct Experiencing of Emotion

Rationale: Engaging With Negative Emotions

In order to begin preparing the client for the direct experiencing of emotion sessions, a brief exposure is conducted to introduce the client to the process of directly experiencing unpleasant emotions and cravings with imaginal exposure. The therapist will gently guide the client through this first exposure to acquaint the client with the procedures. To build the client's confidence, the therapist will direct the client in the use of a coping skill for reducing within-session distress and craving. This approach is intended to show the client that behaviors other than drinking can be used to manage uncomfortable emotions and cravings. During future sessions, the exposure duration will be extended and the negative emotional drinking situation will include more details designed to increase the client's engagement with negative emotions and craving for alcohol.

> *As we discussed previously, unpleasant emotions play a role in a number of unhealthy behaviors including drinking. Many people report drinking when they experience unpleasant emotions such as anger, sadness, boredom, anxiety, or frustration. In addition, many people relapse in situations involving uncomfortable emotions and*

conflicts with others. Therefore, it is important to learn healthier ways of managing unpleasant emotions.

It is natural for people to want to escape or avoid unpleasant emotions, physical sensations, and cravings. However, problems arise when people begin to rely on alcohol as a way to cope with these uncomfortable experiences. We know that every time someone feels an uncomfortable emotion and then drinks, drinking is reinforced or strengthened as a way to cope with problems. Although avoiding these uncomfortable experiences may provide some relief in the short term, it actually prolongs the uncomfortable emotions and cravings, which can interfere with recovery from alcohol problems. As you may have discovered, when emotions or cravings are suppressed or pushed away, they tend to resurface or return and may become even stronger. However, by engaging or "staying with" uncomfortable emotions, sensations, and cravings, you will notice that they often become less intense over time.

To help you learn to stay with and manage these uncomfortable feelings, we use an imagery technique in which we will ask you to imagine a drinking situation that also involves uncomfortable emotions. Using imagery, we go through the situation step-by-step, practicing ways to manage the discomfort and get through it without drinking. We will do that in session where you have support and encouragement, and the safety of no opportunity for drinking.

We have found this technique to be effective in reducing the intensity of the uncomfortable emotions and the urges and cravings that often go along with them. You will learn that uncomfortable emotions and urges to drink are temporary and that when you allow yourself to experience them without avoiding or suppressing them, they will pass. You will deepen your awareness and understanding of the thoughts, emotions, and sensations that precede drinking for you. Finally, you will learn new ways to manage your high-risk drinking situations and then have a chance to practice them. Knowing that you can successfully manage your emotions and cravings will provide you with confidence that you can get through these situations without drinking.

All of these reasons come together to help you better manage unpleasant emotions that could otherwise lead to drinking. The goal is for you to feel that you are in control when experiencing unpleasant emotions, instead of feeling that your emotions are controlling you. Another goal is for you to experience and tolerate uncomfortable emotions, sensations, and cravings without feeling a strong need to escape or avoid them by drinking or engaging in another type of unhealthy behavior. Today and during the next 3 sessions, we will ask you to imagine yourself in situations that involve uncomfortable feelings that you generally seek to avoid or escape by drinking, and *you will imagine yourself experiencing these situations and all of the emotions that go along with them, while getting through them successfully without drinking.*

Before we move on, do you have any questions?

Rating Scales

The client's level of distress and craving are monitored every 3 to 5 minutes during imaginal exposure. Record the ratings on the Direct Experiencing of Emotion Recording Form (Appendix D of this guide). These ratings will enable you to monitor changes in emotional distress and craving levels associated with specific parts of the negative emotional drinking situation. Importantly, you can monitor the client's level of emotional engagement and the intensity of urges or cravings. By tracking both distress and craving levels simultaneously, you will see how the client's levels of emotion and craving are related. This information can be shared with the client to illustrate progress in treatment. There are two ways in which the ratings show progress in treatment. First, both emotion and craving ratings decrease over successive exposures. This is illustrated by lower peak levels of responding and by less exposure time to reach these low rating levels. Second, you may see evidence of greater separation between the client's distress ratings and craving. Specifically, the client's level of emotional distress no longer elicits a strong craving response. This demonstrates to the client the weakened connection between emotions and drinking and underscores the client's confidence in their ability to "ride out" the emotion without drinking.

We know that over time, emotions and urges to drink can change in how mild or intense they are. Emotions and urges can start small and become quite strong before they go back down again—like the wave we have talked about. As you keep working on managing and regulating emotions without drinking, you'll notice that these emotions and urges to drink become less intense. Using our wave analogy, the waves don't crest as high. As we begin to work together on the imagery scenes, it's important for us to monitor the intensity of your emotions and desire to drink. To do this, we use rating scales. This helps us stay aware of the feelings and cravings, makes it easier to track how they change over time, and allows us to keep track of the progress you are making.

Individual Distress Scale:

In order to monitor changes in your level of emotion during the imagery scenes, we need to use a scale that is familiar to both of us. The individual distress scale below has numbers from 0 to 100 and indicates your level of discomfort. A rating of 100 indicates that you are extremely upset, the most you have ever been in your life; a rating of 0 indicates no discomfort at all, or complete relaxation. Often when people say they have a rating of 100, they may be experiencing physical reactions such as sweaty palms, palpitations, difficulty breathing, and feelings of dizziness. This scale is personalized to include examples of situations from your own life that elicit different levels of discomfort at each point on the scale.

Here is an example of one person's scale:

0 = watching TV in bed, very relaxed
25 = walking down the street during the day
50 = at home alone during the afternoon
75 = getting a phone call from my child's teacher
100 = like I felt when my partner left me

Using the Individual Distress Scale (Appendix C of this guide) identify personal situations for each of the 0, 25, 50, 75, and 100 scale points on this distress scale. This should take no longer than about 5 minutes.

Craving Scale:

We will also be monitoring the intensity of your craving or urge to drink with 0 being no craving at all, and 100 being the strongest possible craving you can have. This is the same scale you have been using for reporting the strength of your cravings on the Daily Monitoring Log.

Direct Experiencing of Emotion Using Imaginal Exposure

Okay, let's get started. Let's review the high-risk drinking situation we talked about earlier. As we do this, it's very important that you do not imagine yourself drinking during the imaginal exposure. You will imagine the part where you experience an urge or craving to drink, that's important, and is part of what makes this work. You will experience the urge as it rises up, peaks, and then subsides. The goal is for you to ride out the urge like an ocean wave without giving in to the temptation to drink. As we have discussed, it's important for you to face your emotions and your cravings and not avoid or escape them by drinking or other means. This includes not drinking "before" or "after" the scene that you are imagining. It's also very important that you don't make a decision during the imagery exercise to "drink later." In our experience, emotion and craving ratings decrease when a person makes the decision to drink. Does that make sense? If you *do go ahead and make the decision to drink, or drink in the scene, the technique will not be as effective and your drinking behavior will be reinforced or strengthened.*

> **TIP** As you begin the exposure scene, if the client seems under-engaged and his ratings of distress and craving are not increasing or have decreased, bring this to the client's attention. Sometimes the client will state that they have imagined themselves having "consumed" a few drinks before entering the imaginal scene. The client may also state that they made the decision to drink at a later point in the scene. At this point, you have two options. First, stop the scene and re-evaluate whether to start the scene at an earlier point in time. That is, before any drinking has occurred. Second, rewind to the point in the scene *before* the decision to drink was made and resume the scene. This time, instruct the client that they are not to decide to drink at a later time because this will reduce the effectiveness of the exposure. Alternatively, you may decide to fast forward the scene closer in time to when the client would drink, and then have the client stay in that moment, focusing on his emotional distress and craving, but not drinking.

Every few minutes, I'll ask you to rate your emotional discomfort or level of distress, and your urge or craving to drink. Without stopping the imagery or opening your eyes, you'll give me a number for both of them. I'll say "Level of distress?" and you'll provide me with a number between 0 and 100 that indicates your level of emotional discomfort. Then I'll say "Craving?" and you'll provide me with a number between 0 and 100 that indicates your level of urge or craving. Let's practice right now. The numbers you indicate should reflect how you are feeling right now as you're sitting here. What is your level of distress right now?

The client should respond with a numerical rating. If the client's response does not include a specific number (e.g., says "pretty high" or provides a numerical range such as "between 25 and 40"), you can repeat back the response and then ask for a *specific* number.

Okay. Your level of distress right now is low. (Adjust wording based on client's response.)
How about your level of craving? How would you rate your level of craving right now?

Again, be sure the client responds with a specific number such as "15" or "65."

> *Okay. Your level of craving right now is low; it's not very strong right now.* (Adjust wording based on client's response.)

Be sure to record ratings for both distress and craving on the Initial Ratings line of the Direct Experiencing of Emotion Recording Form (Appendix D).

> *Let's get started. Make yourself comfortable. This will work best if you close your eyes. I am going to ask you to picture this scene as if it were really happening to you right now. Allow yourself to fully experience any feelings you're having, remaining in contact with them, without trying to suppress them or push them away. I will ask you to take me through this event step-by-step, telling me what you see, hear, and feel; telling me everything that is going on as it is happening.*

Place the client in the scene by reading a brief description of the negative emotional drinking scene that was constructed at the end of the last session.

> *Picture this as if it were really happening to you right now.*

Therapist statements that encourage the client to "stay with" the uncomfortable emotions and sensations include:

- *You're feeling _____* (use the client's own words for emotional discomfort).
- *Describe how that feels.*
- *Your chest hurts (reflecting client's description). Focus on your chest and what that feels like.*
- *Good, you're allowing yourself to feel _____ (client's words for emotion). Keep going.*

Listen as the client goes through the scene, providing prompts and encouragement as needed, asking for distress and craving ratings approximately every 3–5 minutes, and recording them on the Direct Experiencing of Emotion Recording Form.
    Sample encouraging statements:

- *You're doing great, let's keep going.*
- *Good, keep going...*
- *Nice job. Hang in there.*

- *You're doing very well. Stay with the emotion.*
- *Great job!*
- *You're doing well, stay with the image; this part's difficult but you're safe here.*

You can prompt for additional cues, repeating those newly obtained cues that are likely to intensify the client's negative affect and urges to drink and noting the cues for use in future exposure sessions. Sample prompts for additional cues include:

- *Where in your body do you feel that?*
- *What are they doing?*
- *How do they look?*
- *What are you doing now?*
- *Where are you in the room?*
- *What do you see? Hear? Feel?*
- *What happens next?*
- *What's the emotion?*
- *How would you describe that?*
- *Where is the alcohol located?*
- *What would increase your craving?*
- *What would increase your emotion?*

If the client is not fully engaged, it may be due to scene selection. In a first exposure session, it is not uncommon for clients to misidentify the timing and location of their peak emotions and cravings. Examples of how to "advance" or "fast forward" the scene include:

- *What happens next?*
- *Tell me when anything changes.*
- *What would increase your level of emotion at this point?*
- *What would increase your level of craving at this point?*
- *Let's fast forward to. . .*

> **Note:** In this first imaginal exposure session we allow the client to engage in a Mindful Breathing exercise in an effort to down regulate the level of distress and craving. The goal is to create a positive first encounter with imaginal exposure and to demonstrate to the client that reducing the intensity of unpleasant emotions and craving are within the client's control. The therapist will assess the client's ratings of distress and craving after one minute of Mindful Breathing, note any changes, and provide the client with positive feedback and encouragement for the effort.

Take the client to the point in the scene *right before* they would typically drink; hold the client in that moment right before any drinking takes place for about 20–30 seconds. During this time, instruct the client to "stay with" the discomfort. Allow for short periods of silence, interspersed with encouragement and questions to elicit more information and cues. When there is approximately 15–20 minutes remaining in the session, prompt the client to move forward in the scene, and allow the client to engage in a minute of Mindful Breathing. This should result in a decrease in both the client's ratings of distress and craving. Ask the client for a final set of ratings and then have them open their eyes. Use the remaining session time to process the exposure with the client and review between-session assignments.

> **TIP** When conducting future exposure sessions, it is important to follow the client's scene until you elicit the specific negative emotion associated with the strongest urge to drink. For example, a client may initially present with a situation that involves having an argument with his partner and the accompanying anger, as precipitating an intense urge to drink. In working through this situation with the client, he describes that his partner has now left the house and he is alone in the basement feeling lonely and sad. He then reports reaching for a beer in the basement fridge. In the process of staying with the situation, slowing down the pace of the scene, and probing gently regarding emotions, physical sensations, and thoughts, the client comes to see that it is not the initial anger during the early part of the argument that fueled the intense urge to drink, but the later loneliness and sadness that initiated the urge to drink. The client comes to discover that loneliness and sadness are important trigger emotions for him and that he drinks in order to avoid or escape these emotions. Again, we want to focus on the unpleasant emotions that are most proximal to the client's craving or urge to drink.

If the client's distress and craving levels remain somewhat elevated after the exposure is completed, then the therapist may intervene to help reduce the client's ratings further. A sample script follows:

> *You did a great job. Let's see if we can bring your levels of distress and craving down a bit more. Without opening your eyes, I would like you to notice your feet on the floor, your back against the chair, your hands resting gently on the arms of the chair or in your lap. Allow yourself to relax and settle into the chair. Now bring your attention to your stomach, allowing it to relax and become soft.*

Focus your attention at the place in your body where you can feel your breath come and go most easily and naturally. Where is that? (Client responds) *You can feel your breath in your _____* (client's breathing focal point). (3-second pause)

Allow yourself to feel the full movement of your breath, in and out of your body. Think to yourself "in" when you breathe in, "out" when you breathe out and "pause" for the space between the breaths. (3-second pause)

Allow your breath to come and go without trying to control it. Let go of any thoughts about the next breath or the last breath. Pay attention to "just this breath." (3-second pause)

Notice if there is tension in your body. Allow your muscles to relax and settle. Let go of any judgments about how you feel. Return attention to your breath. (3-second pause)

Just breathing. (3-second pause)

When you are ready, you may open your eyes.

What is your level of distress?

What is your level of craving?

Record the final ratings of distress and craving on the Direct Experiencing of Emotion Recording Form.

Processing of Direct Experiencing of Emotion

Engage the client in a discussion of their experience with the imaginal exposure scene. Ask the client what the experience was like and be prepared for responses such as feeling "sleepy," "relaxed," "weird," or "different." Probe for and reflect back any response that indicates a decrease in unpleasant emotion and craving. Provide your own observations of the client's distress and craving ratings during the scene.

Select from the following sample questions and statements exploring the client's experience:

You're feeling _____ (client's response). You did it. You let the emotion and craving pass without drinking. What was it like to get through that situation without drinking?

- *What was this experience like for you?*
- *Although this was the first time, you have begun to weaken the connection between your emotions and drinking. That takes some real inner strength.*
- *What do you think about how the distress and desire to drink passed?*

- What did you notice about your emotions? Your physical sensations? Your thoughts?
- What else did you notice?
- Do you have any questions?

At this point, assess the client's rating of distress and craving to ensure they are low.

- What are your ratings now? Your level of distress? Your craving?

Between-Session Skill Practice

- Identify a Dedicated Mindfulness exercise to practice for 3–5 minutes, two or three times per day.
- Practice Mindful Moments five times per day.
- Observe any emotions related to the negative-affect drinking scene.
- Record efforts to cope with any unpleasant emotions.

It's common for clients to think about the exposure scene between sessions. Alert the client to this possibility and let them know that you will want to review any between-session thoughts or emotions at the next session.

> So often in life we keep thinking about something that has happened, which can provide us with an additional opportunity to process it and learn more about ourselves. I would like you to keep thinking about this negative emotional drinking situation that we focused on today. In particular, I would like you to pay attention to the thoughts, feelings, or physical sensations that you experience. You can use your Daily Monitoring Log to write them down. We will review them next time we meet.

- Complete the Daily Monitoring Log.
- Continue to fill in the high-risk situations, coping plans, and list of supportive people in your Personal Coping Plan.

Making It Happen

- Build it into daily life.
- Think about when and where to rehearse skills.
- Uses reminders and cues to practice the skills.

Chapter 11

Session 8

Enhancing Social Support Networks and Direct Experiencing of Emotion

Materials

Managing Negative Emotions Without Drinking workbook, Chapter 10

Therapist brief mindfulness exercise scripts, located in Chapters 5, 6, and 7 of this book

Therapist Form: Direct Experiencing of Emotion Recording Form (Appendix D)

Therapist Form: Scene Development worksheet, extra copies (Appendix B)

Client's scene information and completed Individual Distress Scale

Client's Personal Coping Plan (workbook, Chapter 9)

Session Overview

In this session, you will discuss with the client deficits in social support often experienced by AUD individuals, the importance of building or enhancing a social support network, identifying personalized social support needs, and developing a plan to strengthen the client's support network. You will continue with the direct experiencing of emotion to a high-risk negative-affect drinking situation. You will introduce the "pause and hold" technique, which allows for the client to remain in contact with portions of the imagery scene that elicits high levels of negative affect or urges to drink in order to provide greater exposure to these imagery cues and enhance emotional processing.

Session Outline

- Session introduction
- Enhancing social support networks
- Direct experiencing of emotion (Session 2 of 4)
- Between-session skill practice

Session Introduction

Conduct Breathalyzer Test

Brief Mindfulness Exercise (3–5 Minutes)

Choose a brief mindfulness exercise or offer the client the choice of any brief mindfulness exercises from Sessions 2–4.

Review Between-Session Skill Practice

If the client continues to experience difficulties engaging in between-session skill practice, work collaboratively to include skill practice into their everyday lives. Use the analogy of ripples in a pond to explain that even one small change can create a ripple effect and result in significant improvements in multiple life areas. See Chapter 3 of this guide for ways to increase client engagement with between-session skill practice.

Reinforce Successful Skill Use and Progress

This can be accomplished while reviewing the Daily Monitoring Log, if desired. Reinforce the client's use of other skills used over the past week or progress towards abstinence.
  Sample questions:

- Are any high-risk situations becoming easier to manage?
- Were there times over the past week when you wanted to drink, but didn't?

Review Daily Monitoring Log

Engage the client in a discussion of the type of high-risk situations they have encountered over the past week, their urge or cravings, skills or strategies they implemented to manage these situations, and the amount of alcohol consumed daily, using standard drink sizes.
  Sample questions:

- How have things been going?
- Over the past week, were there times when you wanted to drink?
- Let's look over the monitoring sheet . . . what were some ratings for your desire to drink?
- Is this a situation in which you tried to abstain? What did you do (skills or strategies) to get through it without drinking?
- How well did this work?

- *What was your drinking like over the past week?*
- *How many standard drinks did you have on that day?*

Provide feedback on skills or strategies the client implemented to manage high-risk situations. Were the skills or strategies used effective? If not, are there alternative skills or strategies from prior sessions that might be more effective? Do any high-risk situations pose a unique challenge, or require additional attention? This is a good opportunity to discuss upcoming high-risk situations that may prove challenging for the client. Listen for situations that could be used in today's exposure session.

Enhancing Social Support Networks

General Information

In this part of the session, you will review basic information with the client on the topic of social support systems. The Skills Guidelines section later in this chapter provides information and considerations to assist clients in taking steps to expand their social support systems including self-help groups.

Social support systems:

- Are comprised of people such as partners, friends, family, and co-workers.
- Consist of different types of support such as general or moral support, information or hands-on assistance.
- Generally are a two-way street with members both giving and receiving support.
- Can be limited for some individuals who are reluctant to seek help because accepting assistance conflicts with a sense of independence or masculinity.
- Instill confidence in a person's ability to successfully manage challenges.

Social Support and AUD

Many problem drinkers have found that their social support networks have deteriorated over the years due to a number of factors including social withdrawal, isolation, or interpersonal conflicts resulting from their alcohol use. Often, their social circles have narrowed to include only other heavy drinkers. When individuals stop drinking, they may feel lonely and miss socializing with their drinking friends. It is especially important to encourage clients to begin meeting new people and initiate building friendships so that they are less tempted to return to social settings in which they drank heavily. Some individuals express awareness that drinking has helped them to socialize and they are uncomfortable meeting new people or socializing without drinking. Some individuals may avoid socializing or meeting people, expressing how difficult this is for them. For most individuals, this avoidance is likely to lead to loneliness, boredom, and feeling isolated, which are common high-risk situations for relapse to drinking.

There are many common stresses that are associated with problem drinking: emotional, interpersonal, financial, vocational, and medical. The client has improved chances of coping effectively if they have a strong social support network. Remaining abstinent, effectively managing problems caused by heavy drinking, and managing high-risk-for-drinking situations are usually more difficult in the absence of social support from others. Reaching out for social support can be especially difficult for clients who feel they have consistently disappointed others and have "burned their bridges."

Skill Guidelines

The following guidelines are intended to facilitate client engagement in a discussion of the types of problems that are amenable to social support, how to identify individuals who are most appropriate and likely to provide support, and how to go about enhancing their social support network.

Building Support: What, Who, and How

Engage the client in a discussion of *what* type of support they would like. This may include the following types:

- **Help with information.** This may include resources, emergency help, or problem solving. The client may need information about local clubs and community activities, apartments for rent, job vacancies, small loans, shelter, basic household or personal items, or transportation. This information can be obtained from individuals who can provide new options and help weigh choices or from someone who has coped with a similar problem.
- **Sober friendships.** For most clients, it is helpful for them to identify individuals who have had alcohol problems in the past and who are now sober or who strongly support the client's abstinent lifestyle. Clients can compare their experiences and reactions to those of sober friends and have someone they can count on for support with their sobriety. Sober friends may provide moral support and encouragement that includes recognition and positive feedback for efforts made towards abstinence, as well as messages of understanding, encouragement and hope. Often, this type of social support can help the client obtain information and identify useful resources.

- **Someone to share the load or help with tasks.** This may include family cooperation with household chores or help from a coworker in completing a job before a deadline
- **Help managing temptation to drink.** These often involve assistance with avoiding or managing high-risk situations and can include asking a spouse or partner to talk with them or participate in a distracting activity when they are craving, asking a friend or coworker not to offer them drinks or talk about drinking when they are around, asking a parent to handle their money or paychecks for a few months so they don't have money lying around that might tempt them to buy alcohol or asking a roommate who drinks not to drink around them.

Work with the client to consider *who* might be most helpful to them. This may include the following:

- **Strong supportive relationships.** Some clients may be able to identify individuals who are already an important part of their social support network and are instrumental in supporting their abstinence.
- **Strengthening existing relationships.** There may be individuals in a client's life who occasionally are supportive or who are identified as potentially supportive. The client may know these individuals or they may be acquaintances who have not yet been approached for assistance but could play a more supportive role. This may include partners, family members, relatives, or friends.

> **TIP** The client should consider carefully whether an individual has the potential to provide support for their sobriety. Some individuals are unlikely to ever be supportive, in which case interactions with them should be minimized or avoided. Some individuals who have not been supportive in the past may become supportive over time, but the client should be advised to exercise caution.

Consider *how* the client can obtain the social support they are seeking. Although dependable relationships take time and effort to develop, the following strategies help to build a social support network:

- **Ask for what you need and be specific.** In order to obtain the support they are seeking, the client should be clear that they are asking for assistance and should be specific regarding the type of assistance needed. Whether this includes help with a task, advice, or moral

support, the more specific and direct the client's request, the more likely they are to be successful in obtaining support.
- **Be an active listener.** When receiving support, it is important that the client pays careful attention and makes sure they hear and understand what is being discussed. Active listening skills include attentive nonverbal behavior such as eye contact, not interrupting, asking clarification questions, paraphrasing back to the person what was heard to ensure accuracy, and responding to the speaker's nonverbal messages such as tone of voice, as well as to the speaker's words.
- **Provide feedback.** It is unreasonable to expect that all of the advice and support provided by the support network will be constructive or useful. The client should begin by thanking the individual for their support while at the same time letting the person know what might be more helpful. For example, "I really appreciate your assistance with helping me think through my choices. I appreciate your suggestions, but what I really need right now is just someone to listen" or "I know you're trying to make me feel better when you say 'It'll all work out,' but it would be more helpful if you could work with me to come up with some ideas for what to do."
- **Lend support to others.** Often, reliable support is a two-way street. A mutually supportive relationship can be more reliable and satisfying than a situation in which one person always gives support and the other always receives it. If the client is ready, initiate a discussion with the client about the possibility of helping someone else. Usually, this benefits the recipient, but it can also strengthen the client's own coping skills.

Expansion of Social Support Network

For many different reasons, a client may find that their current social support network does not provide the kind of help they need to maintain abstinence. This is particularly true if the client's social network does not include individuals in recovery or the client is not involved in self-help groups. The expansion of their social support network may be indicated. This can provide the client with information regarding what to expect during the process of recovery or they may simply wish to obtain additional moral support. When the opportunity arises, requesting help from someone may open the door to a new supportive friendship.

Self-Help Support Groups

Although not all clients will be open to the possibility of becoming involved in self-help groups, they can be a valuable source of support for some people. Groups such as Alcoholics Anonymous (AA) (www.aa.org)

and Narcotics Anonymous (NA) (www.na.org) have been around for many years and have helped thousands of people maintain their sobriety. Alcoholics Anonymous groups can be found in virtually every city in the United States. It is recommended that a client sample at least three meetings, preferably at different locations. Most meetings have a unique "culture" and it can take several attempts for a client to find a group that fits their needs.

Talk with the client about their perceptions and experience with AA while assessing their willingness or concerns about attending. There are several questions you can ask to explore this:

- *What has been your experience with AA?*
- *What did you like about it?*
- *What didn't you like about it?*
- *How many meetings have you attended? Fewer than five? More than five?*
- *What kind of meeting did you attend? Open? Closed? Mixed gender?*

For clients who express reservations regarding the spiritual aspects of AA, you can discuss secular alternatives such as SOS (www.sossobriety.org), Rational Recovery (www.rational.org), and SMART Recovery (www.smartrecovery.org). These websites provide information regarding local and online meetings. Let the client know that, ultimately, the decision as to whether to attend a self-help group lies with them.

In-Session Skill Practice: Enhancing Social Support Networks

Using the Enhancing Social Support Networks guidelines located in Chapter 10 of the client workbook, identify the types of support needed, who might provide the support, and how the client might go about obtaining the support they need. Have the client begin working on the Enhancing Social Support exercise on the following page of the workbook. Conduct a brief role play with the client in which they ask for a particular form of support from an identified person. If the client is having difficulty, the therapist can model ways to ask for support.

> *Okay, so that's how you might ask this person for their support. Let's have you give it a try.*

Provide the client with feedback and encouragement for well-executed skills. Gently suggest alternative phrasing or actions for ineffective strategies.

Direct Experiencing of Emotion

Spend a few minutes eliciting the client's thoughts or reactions to participating in the first imaginal exposure scene during the previous session. Look for signs that the client may be uncomfortable revisiting the negative emotional drinking situation and reporting emotions and cravings during the imaginal exposure. If the client expresses difficulty with some aspect of their experience, then attempt to understand where in the imaginal exposure scene they are struggling, remind the client that this is a safe place in which to express emotions, and ask what you can do to help them through today's exposure. Some steps you could take to facilitate engagement are:

- Validate the client's reactions.
- Have the client talk about the scene content and where the client struggles.
- Suggest conducting today's exposure with open eyes.
- Restate the rationale and reasons for the technique's effectiveness.
- Suggest using Mindful Breathing to modulate the client's emotion and craving responses.

When re-engaging a client who is ambivalent about continuing with imaginal exposure, assess the client's perceived benefits and costs of continuing. Keep in mind that the client's hesitation may reflect avoidance of the emotional content elicited during the last session. Attempt to understand the emotions your client may be avoiding. They may or may not be the same emotions elicited in the imaginal scene. For example, the client may express fears about the therapist's reaction to the client's display of emotion. The client may feel embarrassed by their show of emotion during the last session and express fears of being rejected by the therapist. Relate these and other concerns back to the rationale for conducting exposure. Ask permission to share some additional information about the benefits of imaginal exposure for managing emotions and cravings. Make it clear to the client that, while you believe they can benefit from this treatment, you understand it is the client's choice about how to proceed.

In this second exposure session, you will be using the "pause and hold" technique. This technique allows the client to slow down and remain in contact with portions of the scene that elicit high levels of negative affect and/or urge to drink. Begin by providing a review of the rationale for the direct experiencing.

In the example text that follows, the client's scene involved predominately angry emotions related to arguments with her husband. The client was able to use mindfulness skills to get through the scene without drinking.

Review Previous Exposure Scene and Discuss "Pause and Hold" Technique

> Last week, we used imagery to work on an anger-related drinking situation. You were able to vividly imagine what it feels like when you want to drink when you are having arguments with your husband. You went through the imagery scene without drinking, and you were able to use your deep breathing and mindfulness as a way to successfully manage your emotion response in that situation. It was uncomfortable for a time, but you remained engaged with your emotions and came out on the other side.
> Do you remember what that felt like?
> How did you feel when you got through it without drinking?

Continue to review the client's previous experience with direct experiencing of emotion. Focus on successful aspects of the initial imaginal exposure session in order to build the client's self-efficacy for tolerating unpleasant emotions. If necessary, the therapist may remind the client of the emotional benefits experienced following the scene.

> Using imagery, you were able to see how things could be different when you're experiencing unpleasant emotions. We only did it once, but even so, you got a chance to work through the high-risk situation without drinking. This starts the process of breaking the connection between unpleasant emotions and drinking. You learned what you could do instead of drinking such as deep breathing and being mindful. You discovered that the unpleasant emotions and urges did pass, and that you could handle the temporary increase in discomfort. You realized that you could get through it without having to drink.
>
> To further weaken the connection between your emotions and drinking, today we will spend some time revisiting the same high-risk drinking situation. Just like last time we will include as many details as we can about what you are seeing, thinking, and feeling. However, in order to further weaken the connection between your emotions and drinking, I will be asking you to slow things down a bit today. One way we can do this is to hold you at the peak of the discomfort a little bit longer. Today, I will ask you to "pause and hold" at the point where your emotions and cravings are most uncomfortable. I'll ask you to give me your distress and craving ratings on the 0 to 100 scale every 3 to 5 minutes. As you pause and hold, I will ask you to focus on what you see, hear, and feel, and then we'll move forward in the scene. This process can deepen your awareness of uncomfortable thoughts, emotions, and sensations that precede drinking for you. With greater awareness, you may no longer feel a need to avoid these

> *feelings by drinking. Instead, you can gain comfort in the knowledge that if you stay with the feelings, they will pass, and that you can manage these situations without drinking. Finally, I asked you to breathe mindfully towards the end of the scene. This reduces any remaining distress or cravings you may have and will help you feel more comfortable as you leave the session. I will ask you to do the same today.*

Once the client confirms a willingness to participate, you will consult the imagery cues that were gleaned from the previous exposure session, prior treatment sessions, discussions, and Daily Monitoring Logs.

Instructional Set for Imaginal Exposure

> *Okay, let's get started. Similar to our last session, every few minutes, I'll ask you to rate your level of distress and urge to drink. Without stopping the imagery or opening your eyes, please give me a number for both of them. I'll just say "Level of distress?" and you'll respond with a number between 0 and 100 that indicates your level of emotional discomfort. Then I'll say "craving?" and you'll respond with a number between 0 and 100 that indicates the level of your craving to drink. Let's try one now. Your numbers will reflect how you are feeling right now as you're sitting here. What is your current level of distress?*

Be sure the client responds with a numerical rating. At times, clients may not respond with a specific number. If this occurs, the therapist should validate the client's response and then ask for a specific number.

> *So your level of distress is a _____ (client's rating).*
> *How about your craving?*
> *Your craving is a _____ (client's rating).*

Record both ratings on the Initial Ratings line of the Direct Experiencing of Emotion Recording Form (Appendix D).

> *Just like the last time, with your eyes closed, you'll imagine the high-risk drinking situation as vividly as you can. Using the present tense, you will describe what you are seeing and doing, as well as your thoughts, feelings, and any physical sensations that you are experiencing. Remember, it's very important that you not "drink" during the imagery scene. Not even "before" or "after" the part you are recounting. It's also very important that you don't make a decision during the imagery exercise to "drink later." To imagine yourself drinking during the scene, or even making the decision to drink at a later time,*

> *can impact your levels of distress and craving. If you do imagine yourself drinking in the scene, the technique will lose its effectiveness and drinking, as a way to manage uncomfortable emotions and cravings, will be reinforced or strengthened. Does this make sense?*
>
> *This time, we'll also "pause and hold" when we get to a part where the emotions are more uncomfortable, to really weaken the connection between your discomfort and your desire to drink. It's kind of like hitting the pause button when you're watching a movie. You just stop and hold there for a bit, and then we'll move forward again. I'll say something like, "Okay, let's hold here for a moment . . ." and I may ask about what's going on in that moment for you. We will stay in that moment and allow time for your ratings of distress and craving to change on their own. It's also common for other thoughts and emotions to emerge when you are engaged in the scene. When this happens, your levels of distress and craving may increase. If this happens, I will ask you to stay with those emotions and to describe your thoughts, feelings and sensations just as before. About 10 or 15 minutes prior to end of the session, I will ask you to rate your level of distress and craving. If one or both remain elevated, I will ask you to stop imagining the scene and to engage in a Mindful Breathing exercise to further reduce your levels of distress and craving. We will end the session by taking a few minutes to process your experience with the imaginal exposure.*

You can briefly review the imagery scene and specific cues discussed during last session. Cues of various types may be added, as necessary, to remind the client of the unpleasant emotional drinking scene. Using the earlier example:

> *The situation we talked about last time involved an argument with your husband. Some of the physical sensations you report experiencing include your hands shaking and your heart pounding, and you felt very angry. Your thoughts included how much you hated him and that you should have divorced him years ago. Thinking this way brought up feelings of loss and sadness.*

Conducting Imaginal Exposure

> *Okay, get comfortable in your chair, close your eyes and imagine this scene as vividly as you can.*

At this point, provide a brief description of the scene, adding cues obtained from the prior exposure session.

> *I would like you to picture this as if it were really happening to you right now. Please allow yourself to fully experience any feelings you're having, remaining in contact with them, without trying to*

suppress them or push them away. Using the present tense, take me through this event step-by-step and tell me what you see, hear, and feel. Tell me everything that is going on as it is happening.

As you listen to the client describe the scene, provide prompts and encouragement as needed, asking for distress and craving ratings approximately every 3–5 minutes, and record the ratings on the Direct Experiencing of Emotion Recording Form. If the client has difficulty gauging their level of distress, you may offer to remind them of their personal anchor points on the 0–100 scale.

Prompt for additional cues that may serve to intensify the client's negative emotions and urges to drink. Use suggestions or questions intended to elicit more details of the scene, repeating any newly obtained details and noting them for use in future exposures by writing them on the recording form. Remember, it is very important to use the client's own words. For example, if the client uses the word "shaky" then repeat "shaky" instead of "jittery" or "on edge." This can impact the client's engagement in the imagery scene. It's also very important that your client not drink in the scene. Drinking is an escape or avoidance behavior that is likely to reduce the level of emotion and craving. Finally, be observant of other behaviors or thoughts that may reduce the client's intensity of emotion or desire to drink.

As the client's distress nears its peak, "pause and hold" at the point where they are experiencing the specific emotion associated with the strongest urge to drink. (Note: It may be a different emotion than the one the client started out the scene with.) Hold the client in that moment, direct their attention to their experience (physiologically, cognitively, emotionally), and ask them what is happening in that moment. Using the earlier example, you can say:

Let's stay right there. Focus on your husband's face; he is sweating. He has "angry eyes." You can hear him yelling. You can't believe he is this angry about a small dent in the car. He is completely out of control. You feel your heart pounding and your hands shaking. You realize how angry you feel. How much you despise him in this moment. Feel your heart pounding . . . your hands shaking. You hear him swearing as he walks outside slamming the kitchen door behind him. You're standing alone in the kitchen, your heart still pounding and your hands feeling shaky. Focus on your pounding heart and shaky hands. You think about how much you dislike him in this moment. You should have left him when you had the chance. As you stand there alone, you notice your anger giving way to a feeling of sadness. You know the vodka is in the kitchen cabinet to your right, and you have an overwhelming urge to drink. Pause and hold right there. Continue to focus on what it's like to feel sad. Stay right in that moment. Tell me what is happening.

As you have the client pause and hold in that moment, remain quiet and allow your client to guide the direction of the scene. Trust that your client knows this scene well. As the therapist, your job is to follow her emotions. Ask the client to tell you what is happening, what they are seeing, feeling, or are thinking. Probe for physical sensations. Reflect her answers back to deepen her engagement with her present moment experience. Assess for level of distress and craving every 3 to 5 minutes, or when you see that the intensity of either response may have changed (higher or lower). Use the Direct Experiencing of Emotion Recording Form and take notes on what the client reports and on any new cues that are introduced into the scene, particularly cues that elicit emotion or craving.

Additional statements that encourage the client to fully experience the emotion as they "pause and hold" include:

- *Let's pause here for a moment. Stay with those feelings.*
- *Stay with the emotions. You can let me know when anything changes.*
- *Stay there, stay with the _____ (client's word choice for the emotion).*

Keep track of where you are in the session. Leave sufficient time (10–15 minutes) to process the scene with the client and assign skill practice. As you approach the end of the session, the client's ratings of distress and craving may still be elevated. If so, you can assist the client in decreasing her level of distress and craving by engaging her in one or two minutes of Mindful Breathing. In this session, you will have spent between 15–30 minutes engaged in the direct experiencing of emotion. If the first exposure was closer to 15 minutes, you may repeat the scene (See the "Second Presentation of the Direct Experience of Emotion Exposure Scene" later in this chapter.) This timing will allow for 10 minutes to process the scene and 5 minutes to wrap-up and assign between-session skill practice exercises.

Post-Exposure Processing

> *As we approach the end of this imagery scene, keep your eyes closed and tell me your level of distress. Craving?*

The therapist records these ratings on the recording form. Reflect any feelings the client may report and note encouragingly that the strongest of the emotions and urges have passed. The client may state that they feel "sleepy," "relaxed," "weird," or "different." Probe for any response that indicates they are experiencing a decrease in negative affect and reflect it back to the client. Following the earlier example:

> *You're feeling much less angry and upset now. Okay, gently allow yourself to open your eyes and stretch if you need to.*

> *You did it; you let the emotion and craving pass without drinking. You faced a difficult situation today. How do you feel about it?*

It is likely that the client's emotion and craving changed during the scene. Take this opportunity to reinforce the idea that emotions and craving are not permanent, and by staying with them, fully experiencing them, and not pushing them away, the emotions change and even decrease. Discuss any barriers to the experiencing of emotions and cravings within the scene. Problem solve and remind the client that this is a safe environment in which to experience these feelings.

> *The act of slowing down and paying attention to your emotions, thoughts, physical sensations, and cravings can reveal a range of experiences that you may not previously have been aware of. Let's take a few minutes and talk about what it was like for you.*

- *What was this experience like for you today?*
- *How was it different from the last time?*
- *What was it like when you paused at the uncomfortable part?*
- *What other emotions did you experience?*
- *Was anything surprising to you?*
- *What did you notice about the relationship between your emotion and craving?*

Reflect the client's responses and support the client's self-efficacy for managing unpleasant emotions and cravings.

> *By allowing yourself to experience the emotion and the craving in the imagery scene, you are beginning to weaken the connection between your emotions and drinking. That takes some real inner strength.*

- *What do you think about how the emotions and cravings passed?*
- *What did you notice about your emotions? Your physical sensations? Your thoughts?*
- *Did you learn anything new about your reactions in the situation?*

At this point, ask the client about their level of distress and craving. This is to ensure that the ratings are at a low level before ending the session:

- *What are your ratings now?*
- *Your level of distress?*
- *Your craving?*

In the unlikely event that the ratings are still high, take time to manage any remaining negative emotions or cravings. Review the skills that you and your client have covered thus far in treatment and have the client choose a skill for managing emotions and/or cravings. Before the client leaves the session, remind them of the list of coping skills for managing thoughts and urges for alcohol.

Second Presentation of the Imaginal Exposure Scene

Time permitting, you may have the opportunity to repeat the imaginal exposure scene. You may begin the scene closer to the part where the ratings are the highest in an effort to shorten the repetition and effectively manage time in session. Follow the instructions for the first scene presentation and post-exposure processing.

If it is clear that the scene is no longer generating significant distress or craving ratings, you can still revisit the scene, letting the client know that repetition is important. During this repetition, include other internal and external cues which may intensify the emotion and desire to drink that your client mentioned during the earlier scene presentation.

> *Take me through this scene again. Remember to tell me everything you see, hear, and feel as it is happening.*

Remember to save 10 minutes at the end of the session for processing the scene and 5 minutes for reviewing between-session skill practice. Then take the final distress and craving ratings to ensure that the ratings are at a low level before ending the session.

Between-Session Skill Practice

- Identify a Dedicated Mindfulness exercise to practice for 3–5 minutes, two or three times/day.
- Practice Mindful Moments five times per day.
- Observe any related emotions to the negative-affect drinking scene.
- Record how you coped with the emotions.
- Observe and note additional situations involving uncomfortable emotions that could serve as the basis for a future imaginal scene.
- Complete the Daily Monitoring Log.
- Continue to fill in the Enhancing Social Support worksheet.

Making It Happen

- Build it into daily life.
- Think about when and where to rehearse skills.
- Use reminders and cues to practice the skills.

Chapter 12

Session 9
Seemingly Irrelevant Decisions and Direct Experiencing of Emotion

Materials

Managing Negative Emotions Without Drinking workbook, Chapter 11

Therapist brief mindfulness exercise scripts, located in Chapters 5, 6, and 7 of this book

Therapist Form: Direct Experiencing of Emotion Recording Form (Appendix D)

Therapist Form: Scene Development worksheet (Appendix B)

Session Overview

In this session, you will assist the client in understanding the concept of seemingly irrelevant decisions (SIDs). These are the small, everyday decisions that people make that can result in a higher risk of relapse to alcohol use. You will work with the client on an in-session exercise to identity SIDs with the goal of minimizing high-risk situations. If decisions made do lead to higher risk situations, developing a plan to mitigate these risks is important. The direct experiencing of emotion is continued in this session with an emphasis on the repeated presentation of portions of scenes that involve "hot spots" or high levels of negative affect or urges to drink.

Session Outline

- Session introduction
- Seemingly irrelevant decisions
- In-session exercise: Apply SID principles to client example
- Direct experiencing of emotion
- Between-session skill practice

Session Introduction

Conduct Breathalyzer Test

Brief Mindfulness Exercise (3–5 Minutes)

Choose a brief mindfulness exercise or offer the client the choice of any brief mindfulness exercises from Sessions 2–4.

Review Between-Session Skill Practice

Collaborate with the client to problem solve barriers that may have interfered with skill practice.

Reinforce Successful Skill Use and Progress

This can be accomplished while reviewing the Daily Monitoring Log, if desired. Reinforce the client's use of other skills they may have used over the past week and progress toward or maintenance of abstinence.
   Sample questions:

- *Are any high-risk situations becoming easier to manage?*
- *Were there times over the past week when you wanted to drink, but didn't?*

Review Daily Monitoring Log

Probe for more details regarding high-risk situations, desire to drink or craving, skills or strategies that were implemented to manage high-risk situations, and the amount of alcohol consumed daily, using standard drink sizes.
   Sample questions:

- *How have things been going?*
- *Over the past week were there times when you wanted to drink?*
- *Let's look over the monitoring sheet . . . what were some ratings for your desire to drink?*
- *Is this a situation in which you tried to abstain? What did you do (skills or strategies) to get through it without drinking?*
- *How did this work?*
- *What was your drinking like over the past week?*
- *How many standard drinks did you have on that day?*

Provide feedback on skills or strategies the client utilized to manage high-risk situations. Were the skills or strategies used effective? If not, are there alternative skills or strategies that might be more effective? Do any high-risk situations pose a unique challenge or require additional attention? Ask about upcoming high-risk situations. Listen for situations that could be used in today's direct experiencing of emotion exposure scene.

Seemingly Irrelevant Decisions

Discuss with the client how the material covered in this session will assist them in meeting their treatment goals. There is a significant amount of material to cover in this session so it should be reviewed at a good pace without detailed elaboration of all the material. However, it is important to keep the client engaged and ensure that they have an understanding of the material by asking questions or eliciting their thoughts on how the session content and skills relate to their particular situation:

> *Our daily lives are filled with many "little" decisions. These can include which route to take when going somewhere, whether or not to make something to eat or buy something already prepared, what to do with extra time, when to do the laundry, and so on. Although these small decisions may not directly involve making a choice to drink, it is possible for them to move you one small step closer to a high-risk situation. Even when alcohol isn't on your mind, it is difficult to always be aware of how a small decision that seems irrelevant to drinking can lead someone into a high-risk situation. Such "small" seemingly irrelevant decisions can allow a high-risk situation to sneak up on you.*
>
> *I have an example here of how a series of seemingly irrelevant decisions led someone into such a high-risk situation. SIDs stands for "seemingly irrelevant decisions," so that's why the person in the example is named SID.*

You can read "The Story of SID" aloud to the client, or alternatively, you can have the client read it aloud. You can initiate discussions at points throughout the story, paying particular attention to the seemingly irrelevant decisions along the way:

The Story of SID

Vignette

Consider this story about SID*, who has an alcohol problem. Imagine him on his way home in the evening after a very long and difficult day. He should have been home hours ago. He feels achy and tired, becoming aware of his parched throat and the gnawing hunger in his stomach. He comes to a traffic light, and it turns red just in time for him to stop. Annoyed, he turns right instead of waiting. This way takes a little longer, but. . . "whatever." He notices a brightly lit sign up ahead. It's the corner store. Wasn't there something he was supposed to pick up? Yes—milk. He decides to stop and pick some up. His stomach rumbles again reminding him to get something to eat while he's in the store. He parks and walks in, automatically turning to the left. Instantly, he sees a sign for his favorite alcoholic drink: "Buy one get one free." He turns around and walks the other way. He picks up some milk, grabs a slightly crumpled premade sandwich, and heads to the cash register. He remembers he has no cash and reaches for his credit card. There is a familiar face at the register. It's Gloria; she always has a smile for everyone. "SID!" she exclaims, "Hey! Your favorite drink is on sale. And I saved a coupon for you—another 25% off!" He puts his items down and hesitates before he says, ". . . Oh . . . thanks, Gloria . . ." He notices the sign that states a $10 minimum is required for using a credit card. Gloria pushes the coupon toward him with an expectant smile. Debating only a second, Sid goes and gets the drinks. They are ice cold in his hands. He imagines cracking one open, and taking a long drink as he sits down in his favorite chair at home. It will be the first of many that night.

***SID**'s name is an acronym for "seemingly irrelevant decisions."

The best approach is to think about every choice you have to make, no matter how seemingly irrelevant it is to drinking. By thinking ahead to the possible options you have and where each of these options may lead, you can often anticipate dangers that may lie ahead. At first, it may feel awkward to consider each decision so carefully, but after some practice it can become second nature and will happen more naturally. It's well worth the initial effort you will have to invest given the increase in control you will gain over your own sobriety.

By paying more attention to the decision-making process, you will have a better chance of interrupting the series of decisions that could lead to drinking. This is important because it is much easier to stop the process early, before you find yourself in a high-risk situation that is difficult to handle. In short, you can catch it before it sneaks up on you. Also, by paying attention to your decision-making process you will be able to recognize certain types of thoughts that can lead to risky decisions. Thoughts like "I have to" go to a party, "I should" see a certain drinking buddy, or "I have to" drive by a particular place. These sorts of thoughts often occur at the beginning of a seemingly irrelevant decision and should be treated as a warning or red flag. Other red flag thoughts often start with "It doesn't matter if I . . .," "I can handle . . .," and so on.

When faced with these daily decisions, choosing a low-risk option to avoid putting yourself in a risky situation is safest. On the other hand, on a rare occasion you may decide to select a high-risk option. If you make this choice, it's smart to plan well in advance how you will minimize your chances of drinking while in the high-risk situation.

By becoming aware of SIDs, you may be better able to take corrective action to avoid an upcoming high-risk situation. It is usually much easier to decide to avoid a high-risk situation before you get too close to it, than it is to resist temptation once you are in the high-risk situation.

As you review the Story of SID, discuss alternative choices that can be made at several of the choice points along the decision tree.

In-Session Exercise: Applying SID Principles

Using a personalized situation elicited from the client, discuss the series of decisions examining some of the "small" choices and how they may lead to a higher or lower risk drinking situation.

Sample prompts to identify and discuss the client's example:

- *Which part of SID's story can you relate to?*
- *What other decisions could you make to reduce the risk of drinking?*
- *If you decide to make a decision that will take you into a higher risk situation, what kind of supports and coping skills could you use to lower your risk?*

Direct Experiencing of Emotion

This will be the third exposure session for the client. During this session, you will again use the "pause and hold" technique as you revisit those parts of the negative emotional drinking situation that elicit more intense emotion and craving.

Review of Previous Direct Experiencing of Emotion Session

Provide a review of the prior session's direct experiencing of emotion exposure. Highlight for the client aspects of the experience in which the client successfully managed the emotion and urge to drink in the imaginal high-risk situation. Review with the client the emotional experience following the imaginal scene.

> *Last week, we used imagery to work on an anger-related drinking situation. You were able to vividly imagine your emotions and your urge drink when arguing with your husband. It was uncomfortable, but you did it. You directly experienced the unpleasant emotions and sensations without drinking. You were surprised that, in addition to anger, you experienced feelings of loss and sadness. You started to think that maybe feelings of sadness were related to your desire to drink in that situation. You also learned that your emotions and cravings increase, peak, and then decrease. Finally, you used Mindful Breathing to further decrease your distress and craving at the end of that scene.*
> *Tell me your thoughts about how this is working for you.*

As the client relates thoughts about the last exposure, determine whether to continue the imaginal exposure using the same situation or whether it would be more useful to switch to a different high-risk drinking situation. Reasons to switch include the client's report of feeling confident to manage the situation without drinking or feeling that they could benefit more from working on a different situation. In the case example provided, the client decided to continue working with the same imaginal scene.

> *Great! The more practice you get experiencing these emotions, the easier they will be to manage without drinking. The connection between discomfort and drinking can be quite strong, so we'll spend our time today repeating the same imaginal high-risk situation we used last time. Every time we repeat it, the connection between unpleasant emotions and drinking gets weaker. So, we'll try to repeat it as many times as we can during our session. An effective and efficient way to do this is to begin at the point in the scene where your ratings of emotion and craving are at or near their peak. You'll stay in that moment until the ratings start to go down and then we'll "rewind," back to the part where your discomfort was the highest. We'll then go through it again, pausing at the top of the "emotional wave," so we can further weaken the connection between your uncomfortable emotions and drinking.*
> *Also, with repetition, the peak intensity of your emotion and craving is reduced. We call this habituation, which is just a technical way of saying the connection between your emotions and drinking is getting weaker. The less intense the emotion becomes, the easier it is to manage the emotions and any urges to drink that come with*

them. You can also think of the repetitions as an emotional push—up, every time you feel discomfort and let it pass, you get stronger.

Check in with the client for her understanding of the rationale. Correct any misunderstandings and address any concerns, if present. Then begin the exposure:

> Just like the last time, I will ask you to rate your level of distress and craving about every 3 to 5 minutes. Also, you don't have to wait for me to ask you, you can tell me at anytime if your emotion or craving is changing. Without leaving the scene or opening your eyes, just say, "my distress is 80," or "my craving is getting weaker, it's a 20." Before we begin the exposure, let's get your baseline levels of distress and craving. What's your level of distress right now? Craving?

Record both ratings on the Initial Ratings line of the Direct Experiencing of Emotion Recording Form (Appendix D).

> Just like last time, I'll ask you to imagine the high-risk drinking situation you have chosen to work on. You'll be aware of what is going on in your body, that is, your physical sensations, emotions, thoughts, and what you are doing. As we do this, it's very important that you not drink at all during the imagery. Not even "before" or "after" the part you are imagining. It's also very important that you don't make a decision during the imagery exercise to "drink later." If you do this, you escape the discomfort and strengthen the connection between emotions and drinking; just the opposite of what this treatment is about. Today, I will ask you to ride out the wave. Instead of using Mindful Breathing or another emotion coping skill, we'll wait for the emotion and craving ratings to decrease on their own.
>
> Like last time, we'll pause or hold when we get to a part where the emotions are more uncomfortable. I'll say something like, "Okay, let's hold here for a moment . . ." Then I'll ask you to describe your thoughts, feelings, and any physical sensations you are experiencing . . . As the wave crests, and your levels of distress and craving begin to decrease, we'll continue to follow the scene to see where it leads. We do this because sometimes different emotions appear that can be quite strong and more distressing than the initial emotion. This secondary emotion is an emotion that we have in response to another emotion. For example, once your ratings of anger peak, you reported having feelings of loss and sadness. We'll spend some time today focusing on those emotions and any relationship they may have to your desire to drink in this situation. If we find that your levels of distress and craving don't change much, or they continue

> *to decrease, then we will rewind the scene, to the point where we started with you back at the top of the emotional wave.*
>
> *We'll do this several times without stopping. We'll keep going as long as the imaginal scene continues to produce fairly strong levels of emotion or craving, or, until you tell me that we've kind of "worn it out," that it no longer elicits a strong emotion or craving response. That will be the best sign that the connection between your emotions and drinking in this situation has been disconnected. With repetition, you also stand to deepen your awareness of the uncomfortable thoughts, emotions, and sensations that occur before drinking for you. With greater awareness you may no longer feel a need to avoid the feelings by drinking. Instead, you will experience that if you stay with the feelings, they will pass. Your sense of self-confidence in your ability to manage these situations without drinking may increase. What do you think?*

Once the client confirms her willingness to participate, you should consult the imagery cues that were noted in the previous session, from discussions, Daily Monitoring Logs, and from the prior exposures. Briefly review the physiological, cognitive, and affective cues and probe for further details only if needed.

Direct Experiencing of Emotion

> *Okay, you can get comfortable in the chair, close your eyes and try to imagine this scene.*

Provide a brief description of the scene.

> *I would like you to picture this as if it were really happening to you right now. Please allow yourself to fully experience any feelings you're having, remaining in contact with them, without trying to suppress them or push them away. Take me through this event step by step and tell me what you see, hear, and feel. Tell me everything that is going on as it is happening.*

Assist the client through one or more repetitions of the scene providing prompts and encouragement. Note both distress and urge ratings about every 3–5 minutes. If new cues emerge, repeat these back to the client in order to intensify the negative affect and urges to drink, noting these cues for use in future exposures by writing them on the recording form. Guide the client through the negative-affect drinking scene by both prolonging and repeating the most intensely negative affect portions, or "hot spots." It is important that the client not drink or engage in any other avoidance behaviors or thinking that may reduce the intensity of the emotion or desire to drink.

Provide encouraging statements throughout the exposure, particularly during times of greater emotional intensity or craving. Continue in this manner until the client's ratings begin to decrease. You may then use the following script to repeat the "hot spot":

> *Your ratings are coming down now. You made it past the peak. You're doing great. Let's keep at it though. Let's see how much you can break free of the unpleasant emotions and your urge to drink in this situation.*
>
> *Let's go back to the part where*_____ (describe a detail to indicate what was happening at the point when the client's ratings were highest (e.g., ". . . you first entered the kitchen").
>
> *You're feeling* _____ (physiological and emotional cues), *and thinking* _____ (cognitive cues). *You can see and hear*_____ (other cues associated with the most intense negative affect in the scene.)

You should continue to collect distress and urge ratings for the second, repeated portion of the exposure, recording them on the form every 3 to 5 minutes. You can begin to wind down the exposure scene once the ratings have begun to decrease on their own. If the second presentation of the exposure scene occurs near the time when the post-exposure processing should occur, and the ratings have not yet come down on their own, use a guided mindfulness activity either in the context of the client's scene or through Mindful Breathing using the following script as a guideline:

> *You can hear, see, and feel everything going on in the scene but at the same time, you know you are here in the room. Keeping your eyes closed, stay in the imagery scene, and take a breath, mindfully. Notice the place in your body where you can feel the breath most easily and naturally. Let your breath come and go on its own. Notice how the breath feels as you breathe in. How would you describe that?* (Repeat back to client.) *How does it feel as you breathe out?* (Repeat back to client.)

> **TIP** If the client's distress or craving rating does not peak above the midpoint, you can discuss with the client ways to intensify their emotions or craving to drink. This may include adjustments to the exposure cues. It can be helpful to ask the client at which point

152 Session 9: Seemingly Irrelevant Decisions

> during the scene was the urge to drink highest. You should assess for other possible barriers and provide reassurance and guidance in overcoming these barriers. For example, you can reassure the client that this is a safe environment in which to experience these emotions, no matter how intense they become. Adjustments to the scene can be made during the exposure, between scene repetitions, or at the end of the session following the exposure processing.

Post-Exposure Processing

Your ratings are coming back down. You made it past the peak again. You're really doing great. Go ahead and open your eyes . . . What was this experience like for you, going through that situation again?

What was it like when you paused at the uncomfortable part?

A little tired from doing those emotional push-ups? I know, it's a work out. Your hard work will pay off.

What was it like when the ratings started going back down again?

You did great! You let the distress and the urge to drink pass. What was that like getting through it without drinking?

What else did you notice?

Did you notice any changes? Did your emotions become stronger or weaker? Was there a change in which emotion you were feeling? When did this happen?

Why do you think an event like this makes you feel so _____ *(feeling)? What is it about* _____ *(the cue) that makes you feel so* _____ *(feeling)?*

I noticed that _____ *(share your observations, which may include the client's desire or attempt to use adaptive coping strategies). I noticed that when you were feeling* _____ *(negative affect), you used* _____ *(adaptive coping). In your daily life, that's better than drinking!*

Following This Session's Final Exposure

How are you feeling?

You did a great job today. You worked hard to break the connection between your discomfort and drinking.

What is your level of distress right now? Your craving?

I can see that you really put in a lot of effort today. I think you made some real progress.

The therapist processes the experience reflecting the client's comments, providing verbal reinforcement, and focusing on the client's experience in imagining and working through the high-risk situation without drinking.

Between-Session Skill Practice

- Identify a Dedicated Mindfulness skill to practice for 3–5 minutes, two or three times per day.
- Practice Mindful Moments five times per day.
- Observe any emotions related to the negative-affect drinking scene.
- Record how you coped with these emotions.
- Observe and note additional situations involving uncomfortable emotions that could serve as the basis for a future imaginal scene.
- Complete the Daily Monitoring Log.
- Complete Seemingly Irrelevant Decisions (SIDs) worksheet.

Making It Happen

- Build it into daily life.
- Think about when and where to rehearse skills.
- Use reminders and cues to practice the skills.

Chapter 13

Session 10

Progress Review, Stimulus Control Strategies, and Direct Experiencing of Emotion

Materials

Managing Negative Emotions Without Drinking workbook, Chapter 12

Therapist brief mindfulness exercise scripts, located in Chapters 5, 6, and 7 of this book

Therapist Form: Scene Development worksheet (Appendix B)

Therapist Form: Direct Experiencing of Emotion Recording Form (Appendix D)

Session Overview

In this session, you will work with the client to review the treatment goals and evaluate progress towards abstinence, while identifying any remaining areas of concern. You will provide the client with information regarding stimulus control of drinking and develop a personalized stimulus control plan. The final imaginal exposure occurs in this session, which will focus on areas of high negative affect or "hot spots." As in the prior session, the post-exposure processing will focus on assessing potential changes in the client's experience of the high-risk drinking situation including emotions, urges or cravings, and self-efficacy to manage these situations without drinking.

Session Outline

- Session introduction
- Progress towards treatment goals
- Stimulus control
- Final direct experiencing of emotion session
- Between-session skill practice

Session Introduction

Conduct Breathalyzer Test

Brief Mindfulness Exercise (3–5 Minutes)

Choose a brief mindfulness exercise or offer the client the choice of any brief mindfulness exercises from Sessions 2–4.

Review Between-Session Skill Practice

Collaborate with the client to problem solve any barriers that may have interfered with skill practice.

Reinforce Successful Skill Use and Progress

This can be accomplished while reviewing the Daily Monitoring Log, if desired. Reinforce the client's use of skills they may have used over the past week and progress toward or maintenance of abstinence.
  Sample questions:

- *Are any high-risk situations becoming easier to manage?*
- *Were there times when you wanted to drink, but didn't?*

Review Daily Monitoring Log

Probe for greater detail regarding high-risk situations, desire to drink or craving, skills or strategies that were implemented to manage high-risk situations, and the amount of alcohol consumed daily, using standard drink sizes.
  Sample questions:

- *How have things been going?*
- *Over the past week, were there times when you wanted to drink?*
- *Let's look over the monitoring sheet . . . what were some ratings for your desire to drink?*
- *Is this a situation in which you tried to abstain? What did you do (skills or strategies) to get through it without drinking?*
- *How did it work?*
- *What was your drinking like over the past week?*
- *How many standard drinks did you have on that day?*

Provide feedback on skills or strategies the client utilized to manage high-risk situations. Were the skills or strategies used effective? If not, are there alternative skills or strategies that might be more effective? Do any high-risk situations pose a unique challenge or require additional attention? Ask about upcoming high-risk situations. Listen for situations that could be used in today's direct experiencing of emotion exposure scene.

Progress Towards Treatment Goals

As we near the end of treatment, I would like to check in with you regarding your drinking goals and progress toward these goals. It's been one month since we last reviewed your progress. The last time we did this, your drinking goal was to _____ (be abstinent or reduce drinking). What is your goal at this time? How would you rate your progress towards this goal?

Following are two options regarding client feedback on progress towards drinking goals. Option A can be used for clients who are still working towards their goals, while Option B can be used for clients who have met their drinking goals.

Option A: *You've made progress, which is really good, but you still have work to do before meeting your goals. After today, we have two more meetings. How would you like your drinking to be different by the end of treatment?*

Option B: *You're right where you want to be—excellent! Looking back over the past 2–3 months, what has been most valuable in helping you reach your goal? Is there something specific that has worked for you?*

Address any remaining client concerns. If possible, suggest one or more skills or strategies previously discussed in treatment or brainstorm with the client to devise a plan to address the problem:

Are there any other problems that we should be paying attention to in treatment?

Are there any issues we should address to help keep things on track for you?

Stimulus Control

At this point, many of the skills that we have discussed have required that you modify your thoughts or behavior as a way to change your problem alcohol use. Today, I would like to talk with you about a way of changing your environment to reduce the risk of drinking. For example, much of our daily behavior is guided by cues in our environment, or "external" cues. A few obvious examples of external cues that guide our behavior would be an alarm clock, a traffic light, or a fire alarm. These cues can signal you to wake up in the morning, cross a busy street, or exit a building. We call this "stimulus control." That's another way of saying that your behavior—say, the behavior of waking up in the morning—is under the control of the alarm clock. If your alarm clock wakes you up and you get to work on time, then your behavior of setting the alarm is reinforced.

Through a similar process of reinforcement, your use of alcohol has likely become associated with a variety of external cues. Simply stated, if you engage in a specific behavior repeatedly in a certain context, over time that context begins to encourage that specific behavior. For example, if you drank frequently while sitting in your living room watching television, you might find that you experience an urge to drink when the TV is turned on. In this example, your drinking behavior is to some extent dependent on your immediate environment, which is the TV room. Other examples of external cues for drinking might be the sight of your usual alcoholic beverage or a neon sign indicating the presence of a bar or store where alcohol can be purchased. Time can also be an external cue. Here's how that might work. Let's say that most days are very structured and Jenn has little time to take a break. When she gets home, she is with her husband and children, who support her abstinence and who she spends time with in the evening. Now let's say that it's the weekend, there is no pressing work for Jenn to do in the house, and her family is spending the day at her in-law's swimming pool. It's almost noon and her family won't be home until late in the evening. She has 8 or so hours of unstructured free time. She thinks about having a drink. In this example, the external cue is the extended period of unstructured time. She used to fill up these extended periods of free time by drinking and she can feel it pulling on her again.

How does this sound to you? Does it make sense?

How might you modify your environment(s) to reduce your risk for drinking?

At this point, the client will either tell you what they have done to modify the environment or they will say that they have not yet done anything of the sort. It's likely that many clients will say that they no longer keep their usual alcoholic beverage in the home. Take note of the things that they have done, providing encouragement when and where you can. Then review other environments they may not have considered as high risk for drinking, as well as other examples of stimulus control that they could implement to reduce their risk of drinking.

Those are some great examples of stimulus control. Basically, this involves making a change in your usual environment to reduce your risk of drinking or to help manage your alcohol cravings.

> Can you think of any other ways in which you could change an environment that previously signaled drinking for you?

Work with the client to elicit examples from their own experiences. If there are no other examples forthcoming, then ask the client if it's okay to share some other examples, one or more of which the client might find useful. Review the list of Stimulus Control Examples provided in the workbook (Chapter 12), stopping every now and then to ask them which ones they would like to implement.

> *Those are really good ideas. I have a list with other ideas that some of my previous clients have found helpful. Although it is the case that what works for one person may not work for another, taking a look at these ideas may help to brainstorm other strategies that might be helpful to you. Would it be okay if we took a few minutes and reviewed the list?*
> *Notice that the stimulus control strategies fall into one of three categories: (1) adding something positive to the environment, (2) removing something that increases risk for drinking, and (3) finding an activity that is either incompatible with drinking or adds a barrier to acquiring or drinking alcohol.*

Direct the client to the updated Menu of Coping Skills and Strategies found in the client workbook.

Direct Experiencing of Emotion

Final Exposure Session

This is the final direct experiencing of emotion exposure session. If the client is still experiencing difficulties engaging in the exposure, explore potential barriers and provide reassurance and guidance in overcoming these barriers. For example, you can reassure the client that this is a safe environment in which to experience these emotions, no matter how intense they become. You can adjust a scene that was used in a prior session or you may decide to move to a new scene if the emotion and urge levels for the scene remain low. It is possible that the scene is no longer able to provoke intense emotion or cravings. You may also decide to move to a new scene if the client appears to be more motivated to work on a recently identified high-risk situation, particularly if prior scenes are not eliciting high levels of negative emotion or urges to drink.

Review of Rationale for Direct Experiencing of Emotion and Instructions

The following sample script contains a review of the rationale for imaginal exposure and includes an explanation of the potential benefits of participating in direct experiencing of emotion. Most clients will benefit from a repetition of the rationale. This will usually take about 2–3 minutes and can enhance their motivation to engage in the exposure. Adjust the script according to the needs of the client. You may provide additional rationale for repeating the scene from the previous session.

> To effectively manage the discomfort and desire to drink in your high-risk situations, our goal is to have you manage these situations without any attempts to escape, avoid, or suppress them or push them away. When you try to avoid urges or cravings to drink and uncomfortable emotions, they can return, often stronger than before. These emotions and cravings are trying to get your attention because they are important and necessary, even the unpleasant emotions. They provide you with valuable information and the energy to make changes or focus on the important things in your life.
>
> We are using imagery to weaken the connection between your discomfort and drinking. You've experienced how both the uncomfortable emotions and urges to drink pass, and how you can get through these high-risk situations without drinking. You've figured out some things to do instead of drinking and you can manage it. You don't necessarily like the feelings, but now you know you can manage them.
>
> During the imagery scenes, we pause and hold at the peak of the emotion and urges in order to speed up the process of weakening the connection between the discomfort and drinking. Every time we do this, the unpleasant emotions lose more of their ability to make you want to drink. When we rewind and repeat the scene, the connection between uncomfortable emotions and drinking gets weaker while your ability to manage the discomfort and urges gets stronger. As you remain at the peak of discomfort—not drinking, planning to drink, or avoiding the discomfort—you become stronger and more confident about being able to manage these situations. As you can see, there are a lot of things at work here when we engage in the imagery scenes.

Assess the client's understanding of the rationale and benefits of the exposure scenes. Determine whether the client is experiencing these potential benefits and has experienced any increase in self-efficacy to manage these high-risk situations:

> How has the use of imaginal exposure helped you to quit drinking and stay that way?
>
> How did you feel when you got through the scene without drinking?
>
> How confident are you that you can manage your unpleasant emotions without drinking?

Session 10: Progress Review

At this point, begin the imaginal exposure of the selected scene:

> *So, let's begin. Remember, every few minutes I'll ask you to rate your emotional discomfort and urge to drink. Without removing yourself from the imaginal scene or opening your eyes, you'll give me a number. The numbers should reflect how you are feeling at that moment.*
>
> *Like last time, you'll imagine that right now you are feeling _____ and want to drink. You'll be aware of what is going on in this situation such as physical sensations, emotions, thoughts, and what is happening around you.*
>
> *What is your level of distress right now? Craving?*

Record both ratings on the Therapist Direct Experiencing of Emotion Recording Form (Appendix D).

> *It's important that during the imagery scene you don't avoid how you are feeling by drinking, making a decision to drink later, or doing anything else to soothe or distract yourself from the unpleasant emotions and your desire to drink.*
>
> *We'll pause or hold when we get to a part of the scene where the emotions are strongest to really weaken the connection between drinking and emotions. You'll just hold there for a moment, and then we'll move forward again. I'll say something like, "Okay, let's hold here for a moment . . ." and I may ask you to describe your feelings and what's happening in the scene. Once you get past the top of the emotional wave where the ratings are the highest, we'll rewind back to the top of the wave without stopping, to get as many repetitions in as we can, to really work at weakening the connection between drinking and emotions. We'll wait for the emotions and cravings to come down on their own, rather than engage in a mindfulness exercise or another emotion coping skill to bring them down.*

Provide a brief description of the scene with a focus on the most relevant cues, probing for more cues, if necessary. If the client's emotion or craving rating is low, discuss changes to the scene cues that may intensify the emotion or urge to drink. It can be helpful to ask the client at which point during the scene the urge was highest. If a different imaginal scene is being used in today's exposure session, try the following:

> *You were successful in working through your high-risk situation during our previous session. You've gotten strong and you've weakened the connection between the unpleasant emotion and the drinking so*

much that it isn't increasing your desire to drink like it did in the past. Congratulations!! You did it!

Given your success, today we are going to practice managing emotions without drinking once again, using a different high-risk situation.

Briefly gather cues for an imaginal scene, recording this information on the Scene Development worksheet (Appendix B).

Direct Experiencing of Emotion

Okay, please get comfortable in your chair, close your eyes, and try to imagine this scene.

Provide a brief description of the scene:

I would like you to picture this as if it were really happening to you right now. Please allow yourself to fully experience any feelings you're having, remaining in contact with them, without trying to suppress them or push them away. Take me through this event step-by-step and tell me what you see, hear, and feel. Tell me everything that is going on as it is happening.

Allow the client to complete one repetition of the scene; record distress and craving ratings every 3–5 minutes. During the exposure, guide the client through the negative-affect drinking scene by prolonging and repeating the most intense negative affect portions, or "hot spots." If time permits, repeat the imaginal exposure scene. You may begin closer to the portion of the scene where the ratings are the highest, in order to maximize the time remaining in session.

Let's try this scene a few more times and see if we can weaken the connection even more. I will have you repeat the scene starting at the part where _____ (point at which ratings are highest).

Keep track of where you are in the session. Leave sufficient time (10–15 minutes) to process the scene with the client and assign skill practice. As you approach the end of the session, the client's ratings of distress and craving may still be elevated. If so, you can assist the client in decreasing the level of distress and craving by engaging the client in one or two minutes of Mindful Breathing. Obtain final distress and craving ratings.

Post-Exposure Processing

The following are sample questions to assist you in processing the exposure experience with the client:

> *Your ratings have come down. You made it past the peak again. You're really doing great. Go ahead and open your eyes . . .*
> *What was your experience like, this time?*
> *What was it like when you paused at the uncomfortable part?*
> *A little tired from doing those emotional push-ups? I know, It's a quite a work out. Your hard work will pay off.*
> *What was it like when the ratings started going back down?*
> *You did great! You let the distress and urge pass. What was that like when you got through it without drinking?*
> *What else did you notice?*
> *Did you notice any changes? Did your emotions get stronger or weaker? Was there a change in which emotion you were feeling? When did this happen?*
> *Why do you think an event like this makes you feel so _____?*
> *What is it about _____ (the cue) that makes you feel so _____ ?*
> *I noticed that _____(share your observations, which may include the client's desire or attempt to use adaptive coping strategies). I noticed that when you were feeling _____, you _____ (adaptive coping). In your daily life, that's better than drinking!*
> *You did a great job today.*
> *What is your level of distress right now? Your craving?*
> *I can see that you put in a lot of effort into the imaginal scenes this session. You really made progress in breaking that connection between your emotional discomfort and drinking.*

Between-Session Skill Practice

- Identify a Dedicated Mindfulness skill to practice for 3–5 minutes, two or three times per day.
- Practice Mindful Moments five times per day.
- Be aware of any additional feelings related to today's imaginal exposure exercise. Note how you coped with the feelings.
- Complete the Daily Monitoring Log.
- Complete the Stimulus Control worksheet.

Making It Happen

- Build it into daily life.
- Think about when and where to rehearse skills.
- Use reminders and cues to practice the skills.

Chapter 14

Session 11
Relapse Prevention and Lifestyle Balance

Materials

Managing Negative Emotions Without Drinking workbook, Chapter 13

Managing Negative Emotions Without Drinking workbook, Chapter 12: Updated Menu of Coping Skills and Strategies

Therapist brief mindfulness exercise scripts, located in Chapters 5, 6, and 7 of this book

Session Overview

In this session, you will provide the client with information regarding the importance of relapse prevention to ensure that the beneficial effects of treatment persist beyond the end of treatment. A discussion of relapse warning signs, including more subtle signs, is intended to promote a daily awareness so that even subtle warning signs of relapse can be recognized and appropriate coping behaviors can be initiated. The importance of lifestyle balance is discussed with the client using the analogy of a rechargeable battery with an emphasis on maintaining a sufficient energy level to manage life stressors. Ensure sufficient positive life activities, including savoring pleasant events, are discussed with the client. The client is engaged in developing a lifestyle balance action plan.

Session Outline
- Session introduction
- Relapse prevention
- Rationale for lifestyle balance
- In-session skill practice: keeping our "batteries charged"
- Between-session skill practice

Session Introduction

Conduct Breathalyzer Test

Brief Mindfulness Exercise (3–5 Minutes)

Choose a brief mindfulness exercise or offer the client the choice of any brief mindfulness exercises from Sessions 2–4.

Review Between-Session Skill Practice

Collaborate with the client to problem solve any barriers that may have interfered with skill practice. See Chapter 3 for further information and strategies.

Reinforce Successful Skill Use and Progress

This can be accomplished while reviewing the Daily Monitoring Log, if desired. Reinforce the client's use of skills they may have used over the past week and progress toward or maintenance of abstinence.

Sample questions:

- *Are any high-risk situations becoming easier to manage?*
- *Were there times when you wanted to drink, but didn't?*

Review Daily Monitoring Log

Probe for details in order to understand high-risk situations, desire to drink or craving, skills or strategies that were implemented to manage high-risk situations, and the amount of alcohol consumed daily, using standard drink sizes.

Sample questions:

- *How have things been going?*
- *Over the past week, were there times when you wanted to drink?*
- *Let's look over the monitoring sheet . . . what were some ratings for your desire to drink?*
- *Is this a situation in which you tried to abstain? What did you do (skills or strategies) to get through it without drinking?*
- *How well did it work?*
- *What was your drinking like over the past week?*
- *How many standard drinks did you have on that day?*

Provide feedback on skills or strategies the client utilized to manage high-risk situations. Were the skills or strategies used effectively? If not, are there alternative skills or strategies that might be more effective? Do any high-risk situations pose a unique challenge or require additional attention? Ask about any possible upcoming high-risk situations.

Relapse Prevention

Relapse prevention, as a treatment approach, is designed to ensure that the benefits of treatment persist well beyond the end of treatment. Following treatment for an alcohol problem, the client will frequently encounter situations or stimuli previously associated with alcohol use. To the extent that the client is able to manage these situations effectively, treatment gains can be maintained.

The first 3 months following treatment for an alcohol problem represent the highest risk period for relapse (Hunt, Barnett, & Branch, 1971). Therefore, it is important that the client continue to practice and use the skills and strategies learned in treatment, so they are available when needed. Practicing these strategies in multiple contexts will strengthen the behavior and make it more likely that they will remember to use one or more of the adaptive strategies in challenging situations.

Review Relapse Warning Signs

Begin the session by providing the client with information regarding relapse warning signs. Direct the client to the Relapse Warning Signs information sheet in the client workbook and allow time for the client to look it over:

> *Changes in thoughts, behaviors, and emotions often occur well before a relapse. Noticing these signs provides an opportunity to intervene and prevent a return to previous drinking patterns. Let's take a look at this Relapse Warning Signs handout. I will give you a minute to look it over. Do you notice any warning signs that may be relevant?*

Engage your client in a brief discussion of any identified warning signs and ask them to think about how they could manage the increased risk for relapse. Relate your client's responses to one or more skills that were discussed in treatment using the Updated Menu of Coping Skills and Strategies located in Chapter 12 of the workbook.

> *It is important to remember that, at times, relapse warning signs can be subtle such as the passage of time or a constant low level of stress that can wear you down over time. Staying alert can take a toll because it requires self-monitoring and self-control. These can be very effortful behaviors. We don't always recognize how stressful it can be to "do the right thing." Sometimes we want to take a "time*

> out" from being vigilant. However, by letting our guard down we become vulnerable to the subtle influence of thoughts, feelings, and behaviors associated with alcohol use. By subtle, we mean that these warning signs can operate in the background, affecting our mood and behavior, but never really grabbing our attention or rising to the level of an obvious warning sign for a high-risk-for-relapse situation.
>
> So, you ask, how can you identify something that is described as almost imperceptible? Well, notice that we are saying "almost" imperceptible. Usually, subtle warning signs can be detected if you take a moment each day to stop and "check-in" with yourself. "Checking-in" doesn't require much effort but it does require that you review or examine your recent thoughts, how you are feeling, and your recent behaviors. This is something that can be done at the end of each day. For example, you might ask yourself the following questions: Did I have any thoughts, behaviors, or feelings today that indicate I may be vulnerable to drinking? If yes, what are they and what can I do to manage them?

Direct the client to the Daily Relapse Prevention worksheet in the client workbook. It can be useful for the client to keep a record of their responses to these questions and identify useful coping skills and strategies in the space provided for days when they feel vulnerable to alcohol use. This can make "subtle" warning signs more obvious and easier to recognize over time. Tracking their responses can be assigned as part of the between-session skill practice.

> Other people who know us well can be good observers of our own behavior and behavior patterns. For example, a family member or friend might say, "Hey, what's going on with you? . . . You don't seem yourself today." or "The last time you were acting this way, you went on a drinking binge." These can be important reminders for you to Stop and Notice your thoughts, feelings, and behaviors. A few minutes spent checking in can make the difference between a lapse or relapse and maintaining your sobriety.
>
> In this treatment program, you have learned a new set of skills that you can use in response to situations that used to signal alcohol use. The key to strengthening these behaviors is to practice them in as many different contexts as you can each day. As you practice each behavior, it will become more automatic and less effortful to engage in the behavior. Eventually, you won't have to think about the new behavior as much, you will just act.

Rationale for Lifestyle Balance

The lifestyle balance portion of this session is intended to review the risks of an unbalanced lifestyle and the benefits of a balanced lifestyle. When an individual's life is filled with demands that drain their energy level and there are few activities that help to build a person's energy reserve, this can increase the risk for relapse to drinking.

> *Today we will discuss another way in which people may move closer to a relapse, and ways to minimize this risk.*

You can use the "Story of SID" from Session 9 to illustrate the connection between an unbalanced lifestyle and relapse.

> *Let's go back to the Story of SID that we discussed a couple of weeks ago. If you remember, he got out of work late: He was tired and hungry. Let me expand on what Sid's everyday life was like, what was going on in his life before he got to the traffic light.*

You can expand on the Story of SID by providing details that emphasize an unbalanced lifestyle such as constant demands, daily hassles, little time to relax, or having too few sources of pleasure. The therapist will include common thoughts such as "I've been good, I deserve this drink" which can lead to a desire to reward oneself with alcohol. Whenever possible, the story details should be chosen so the client can relate to the unbalanced lifestyle. For example, if imbalance in the client's life is largely due to boredom from having large amounts of unstructured time, the details of the relapse story should reflect this rather than reflecting a person who is experiencing too many life demands.

Sample questions to guide the discussion:

- *When Sid pulled up to the light, how was he feeling?* (i.e., tired, hungry, overworked)
- *What was going on in Sid's life that set the stage for a relapse?*
- *What was missing in his life?*
- *What might have happened if Sid had ____* (Provide examples of positive lifestyle choices such as eating well, leaving work on time, getting enough sleep, and engaging in pleasurable activities that can help individuals to "recharge.")
- *How might this story have turned out differently if Sid had spent time noticing pleasant moments throughout the day, thinking back to positive events or anticipating future positive events?* (i.e., savoring)

> *This story illustrates that the way in which people go about making decisions in their everyday lives can make a difference in keeping their lives in balance and maintaining abstinence. When Sid pulled up to the light, he was tired and "running on empty." Unfortunately, none of us have an unlimited supply of energy. Our energy level can*

be viewed as a battery that needs to be charged on a regular basis. If our battery is running low much of the time, we might say our lifestyle is "out of balance."

The extent to which our batteries might need to be recharged can vary from day-to-day, so it's important to check our energy level each day. We don't have an indicator like our electronic devices do. Also, people differ from one another in terms of what kind of activities use energy, and which activities might act as a "recharger."

- *What is it like when people run low on energy?*

Assist the client in generating a few examples in response to this question such as being tired, irritable, impatient, bored, restless, dissatisfied, or finding it more difficult to resist temptation. In addition, people generally begin skipping tasks that take effort now but provide a benefit later. Try to elicit some examples of these effortful but beneficial tasks that are personally relevant for the client. These can include preparing healthier food, calling a friend back, filling the gas tank in the car before it's empty, putting junk mail directly into the recycling or shredder, or preparing clothes for the next work day.

- *How might a low energy level affect a person's ability to maintain abstinence?*

Elicit examples from the client. These can include making a decision not to use a coping skill because they feel too tired and it is easier to give in to cravings for alcohol, thoughts such as "The hell with it!," "I deserve this, I've worked hard!," a need for a reward or a "pick-me-up," not thinking ahead to maintain an awareness of possible SIDs or of early warning signs of possible relapse.

> **Note:** Implementing a change in one's behavior or engaging in self-control requires effort. This effort can drain a person's energy level. Initially, the effort of this new behavior might be high, but over time it generally requires less effort as it is practiced and becomes part of a routine. Right now, a behavior such as drinking is highly practiced and may require little effort. In contrast, a new behavior that takes the place of drinking may require more effort at first, but will take less effort over time. Importantly, fatigue can have a negative impact on the successful performance of a desired self-control behavior such as limiting or abstaining from drinking, thus highlighting the importance of lifestyle balance to keep one's batteries charged.

In-Session Skill Practice: Keeping Our Batteries Charged

In order to keep our batteries charged and prevent a return to drinking, there are a few things you need to know: (1) when it's time to take action, (2) which action to take, and (3) deciding to take action.

Guide the client in a discussion to identify personal "low-charge" warning signs, and ways to increase the client's charge or energy level. The client can begin recording information from the in-session, skill practice on the Lifestyle Balance Worksheet.

1. **Monitor** *your battery (know when).*

    - Check your charge: Make it a point to "Stop and Notice" how you are doing each day.
    - Know the signs that you are running low on energy (personal "low-charge" warning signs).
    - What are the signs that you are running low on energy?

2. **Identify** *some ways to increase your "charge" or energy level (know what to do).*

For each point below, work collaboratively with the client to first generate general examples, then prompt the client to identify personal examples.

In order to identify ways to increase your energy level, it's helpful to first give some thought to what uses your energy to see if any adjustments need to be made. Then we'll review some ways to "recharge."

- What kinds of things **use your energy**? These can be positive or healthy activities such as work, parenting, or relationships. They can also be unhealthy or stressful activities such as a toxic work environment, unhealthy relationships, or daily hassles such as traffic jams.
    - Is there anything in your life that is using too much energy? If so, what could you change or adjust?
- What kinds of activities help people to **recharge**? These can be interesting, pleasant, or meaningful activities that include leisure or recreational activities, self-care activities such as adequate sleep, good nutrition, regular physical activity, or obtaining social support. It may be helpful to identify where you could benefit from a change or an addition to your life. Remember, even small adjustments can eventually lead to significant life changes over time.
    - What could you add or adjust in your life to improve your ability to recharge?

- *Savoring pleasant experiences is another way "recharge" your energy level. Savoring is an emotion regulation skill that enhances and extends pleasure from our positive life experiences. Savoring strategies include consciously directing attention to an ongoing pleasant experience (i.e., during Mindful Moments), vividly remembering past or anticipating future positive events, and sharing positive moments with others.*

    - *What upcoming events or past experiences can you savor to help you recharge?*

Work with the client to select an experience that can be savored in this week's upcoming Mindful Moments practice.

3. *Let's talk about a plan for increasing activities and experiences that could help you to recharge (take action!).*

Work with the client to complete the Lifestyle Balance Action Plan. The focus of the plan is to identify recharge activities and develop a plan to increase these types of activities. Be sure that the plan includes the steps necessary to bring about the desired change. It is important that steps in the action plan are specific and attainable for the client. In the interest of time, this action plan can be initiated in session and finished as part of the upcoming week's skill practice.

- *In order for you to begin _____ (recharge activity), what needs to happen first? What is the next step?*

Between-Session Skill Practice

- Identify a Dedicated Mindfulness skill to practice for 3–5 minutes, two or three times per day.
- Practice savoring during Mindful Moments 5 times per day.
- Complete the Daily Monitoring Log.
- Choose a method for tracking responses to the daily question "*Did I have any thoughts, behaviors, or feelings today that indicate I may be vulnerable to drinking?*" and begin tracking during the upcoming week.
- Complete and carry out the Lifestyle Balance Action Plan.

Making It Happen

- Build it into daily life.
- Think about when and where to practice skills.
- Use reminders and cues to practice the skills.

Chapter 15

Session 12
Accomplishments and Future Directions

Materials

Managing Negative Emotions Without Drinking workbook, Chapter 14

Therapist brief mindfulness exercise scripts, located in Chapters 5, 6, and 7 of this book

Form: Relapse Prevention Plan (Appendix E)

Session Overview

In this final session, you will conduct a review of progress in treatment with the client. You will focus on a review of effective skills and strategies for managing high-risk situations, use of emotion regulation skills for managing negative affect, urges or cravings to drink, and physical sensations. Review and reinforce progress towards meeting drinking goals. You will work collaboratively with the client to complete a relapse prevention plan that will include identification of the client's personal relapse warning signs, preferred skills for managing high-risk situations, identification of social supports for abstinence and any additional treatment needs. It can be helpful to your own work to elicit clients' feedback on positive and negative aspects of treatment and to identify any changes they would make to the treatment. Saying goodbye can be difficult for some clients, so be sure to leave sufficient time in the session to process any emotional reactions the client may be experiencing.

> **Note:** The word *termination* is used to describe the process of concluding treatment and ending the therapeutic relationship in a healthy manner. However, this term may have other negative connotations for the client. As a result, you may choose to use alternative terms such as *wrapping up*, *treatment progress review*, or *next steps*.

Session Outline

- Session introduction
- Review of skills
- Review progress towards effectively managing high-risk situations and drinking
- Review progress managing uncomfortable thoughts, emotions, and physical sensations
- Reinforce progress towards drinking goals
- Expect temporary increases in alcohol-related thoughts and cravings
- Review relapse prevention plan

Introduction

Conduct Breathalyzer Test

Brief Mindfulness Exercise

Choose a brief mindfulness exercise or offer the client the choice of any brief mindfulness exercises from Sessions 2–4.

Review Between-Session Skill Practice

Collaborate with the client to problem solve any barriers that may have interfered with skill practice.

Reinforce Successful Skill Use and Progress

This can be accomplished while reviewing the Daily Monitoring Log, if desired. Reinforce the client's use of other skills they may have used over the past week and progress toward or maintenance of abstinence.

Sample questions:

- Are any high-risk situations becoming easier to manage?
- Were there times when you wanted to drink, but didn't?

Review Daily Monitoring Log

Engage the client in a discussion of the type of high-risk situations they have encountered over the past week, intensity of desire to drink or craving in these situations, and the skills or strategies that were implemented to manage these high-risk situations. If alcohol was consumed, review the amounts using standard drink sizes.

Review of Skills

Begin this session with a review of coping skills the client has learned during treatment. Ask the client how they would respond to uncomfortable emotions or urges and cravings that may arise in high-risk situations. The goal of this exercise is to promote the client's self-efficacy for managing high-risk situations beyond treatment.

Review Progress Towards Effectively Managing High-Risk Situations and Drinking

Begin with an open-ended question regarding how their life differs now as compared with their life prior to entering treatment. Then follow up with several more specific questions that elicit information about the characteristics of their personal high-risk situations, effective skills and strategies for managing urges and cravings for alcohol, and for effecting changes in alcohol consumption:

Sample questions:

- *Looking back, what have you learned about your drinking triggers?*
- *What have you learned about effective methods for managing your urges and cravings for alcohol?*
- *What have you learned here that was helpful to you in making changes to your alcohol use?*
- *What will you take away from this program that will be helpful in the future?*
- *Did this treatment meet your expectations? What would you want to be different?*

Review Progress With Managing Uncomfortable Thoughts, Emotions, and Physical Sensations

This provides an opportunity for you to review the client's progress regarding their understanding of the relationship between thoughts, emotions, physical sensations, and alcohol use, and their ability to manage negative-affect drinking situations.

Sample questions:

- *What have you learned about the relationship between unpleasant thoughts, emotions, and physical sensations, and your use of alcohol?*
- *What have you noticed about the intensity of unpleasant emotions you experience in certain situations?*
- *What have you learned that will help you face future unpleasant emotional high-risk situations?*

Reinforce Progress Towards Drinking Goals

It is important to acknowledge and reinforce gains the client has made during treatment. This is usually straightforward for clients who have made significant changes in their drinking and are now abstinent. However, for those clients who have struggled to make drinking-related changes, reinforcing the gains they have made can be important for the client's self-efficacy to maintain these gains, and possibly, to continue to making additional gains following treatment. Use the following text to guide such a discussion:

> *You're feeling really good about the way you are managing emotions and situations when it comes to drinking. You no longer feel like you have to immediately react in response to emotions and cravings. What strikes me is how different this is from where you began. Four months ago you were drinking _____ (frequency) and having _____ (amount) standard drinks a day. In the last few weeks, you had about _____ (amount) standard drinks on _____ (frequency) days each week. In other words, your alcohol consumption is much reduced and you're beginning to think that you can give it up all together! Now you know what to do if you experience an urge. Experiencing an urge doesn't inevitably lead to drinking. You're able to face these urges and cravings knowing that they will pass. The same is true for unpleasant emotions. You've learned that avoiding unpleasant emotions can make things worse. You have made significant changes in how you manage these situations.*
>
> *There were times when you felt discouraged during treatment but you stuck with it and completed the treatment. You're persistent. You took steps and made positive changes.*

Expect Temporary Increases in Alcohol-Related Thoughts and Cravings

Explain to your client that a return of alcohol-related thoughts, physical sensations and cravings may occur during times of increased stress or when experiencing unpleasant emotions. There is no cause for alarm and this doesn't mean that the effects of treatment are diminishing. It is normal to have these uncomfortable reactions return and it may catch them off-guard. Therefore, it's important to expect that this might happen and that emotions and cravings are like waves that rise up, crest, and then subside. If and when such responses return, the client can use them as a cue to "Stop and Notice" what is happening in their life that may be causing these uncomfortable thoughts and sensations. It may be an early warning sign that some part of their life is out of balance and that greater lifestyle balance is needed.

Review Relapse Prevention Plan

The Relapse Prevention Plan worksheet summarizes the client's highest risk situations and includes their preferred skills and strategies for coping with these situations. The following text provides an example for summarizing this information:

> *Coming home from work has been a time when you have typically felt like drinking. It has been one of the most challenging situations for you to remain abstinent. Your plan is to communicate more frequently with your husband during the day by letting him know when you're leaving work and when you expect to be home, to avoid any detours to pick up alcohol. You also mentioned using the Mindful Breathing exercise when you become aware of negative thoughts about yourself, the kind of thoughts that typically come before a drinking episode for you.*

Probe for additional high-risk situations, early warning signs, and associated coping skills.

> *What else would be a good idea for you to think about ahead of time, in order to prevent a return to drinking?*

Add early warning signs from Session 11 to the Relapse Prevention Plan. (Refer to the Relapse Warning Signs information sheet in client workbook, Chapter 13). Incorporate into the plan skills or strategies the client is likely to use to cope with warning signs. It can be helpful to generate the names of at least one support person the client could turn to, when needed.

Mobilize the client to follow through on their relapse prevention plan.

- *Are you willing to give this a try?*
- *What would be a first step?*

It can be helpful to troubleshoot possible barriers to implementing the plan. Discuss challenges the client may encounter along the way, choosing an example from their Relapse Prevention Plan.

> *Alright, but imagine a situation where your husband is going out to dinner that evening for a work function and won't be home until much later in the evening. You're driving home at 3:30 p.m. It was a stressful day and you suddenly have six or so hours before your husband comes home. What other skills or strategies could you use to maintain abstinence?*

An alternative method for troubleshooting these high-risk situations is to have the client identify a situation that is most likely to pose a challenge to remaining abstinent. Keep in mind that the highest risk situation a client identifies (e.g., death of a parent) may not be the most imminent or frequently occurring situation. You want to identify a situation that has the potential to occur with some frequency. Which situation or event concerns them the most? Engage the client in identifying a situation that is most likely to pose a risk for relapse . . How might this situation occur? What would the situation look like? Would it jump out at them? Would it be slow to develop? These types of questions have relevance for developing a specific plan of action to prevent a relapse. Add these situations and potential solutions to the Relapse Prevention Plan.

For those clients that may require additional treatment services now or in the near future, discuss your recommendations with the client and provide a list of treatment referrals.

Feedback on Treatment

As time allows, obtain feedback from the client about the treatment experience. Encourage the client to speak candidly about both the positive and negative aspects of treatment. Often, this can be framed as information that you seek from all clients with the goal of improving alcohol treatment. Sample questions include:

- *What did you like most about treatment?*
- *What did you like the least about treatment?*
- *What would you change about the treatment?*
- *Is there something you would like to see offered as part of treatment, that wasn't?*

Saying Goodbye

Take time to say goodbye to your client. Comment on your client's strengths and the things you have enjoyed most about working with them. Terminating any relationship in life can bring up emotions for both you and your client so be sure to leave sufficient time to process this with the client.

Appendix A

Common Barriers to Mindfulness Practice

Clients commonly encounter one or more barriers to the regular practice of mindfulness. Multiple barriers may be present simultaneously or occur consecutively, one after the other. Addressing barriers to mindfulness practice is considered a normal part of treatment to which therapists should respond with diligence and patience.

Use the following guidelines to help you identify the reasons why a client may be struggling to incorporate this vital practice into everyday life, and intervene appropriately to support the client's success.

1. Interested in Mindfulness but Has Difficulty Remembering or Completing Mindfulness Practice

Clients who present with this barrier seem motivated and interested in practicing mindfulness on a daily basis. They usually leave the session with every intention of practicing mindfulness just as assigned in the between-session practice, only to return the following week with few instances of successful follow-through. For many clients, this may be a recurrent theme in their lives, making it even more important to provide the support they need in order to bring about this behavior change.

To address this barrier, it is especially important to establish an atmosphere that is conducive to productive problem solving. Begin by normalizing the client's difficulties with completing between-session mindfulness practice, and emphasize that investigating potential barriers to practice is considered part of the treatment process. Guide a collaborative discussion intended to shed light on the factors that might be impeding regular mindfulness practice, brainstorm solutions, and select one or two mindfulness exercises for the following week. For clients whose struggles appear to fit the description for this barrier, the difficulties in carrying out the mindfulness practice may be related to several factors: (1) remembering to engage in mindfulness practice, (2) remembering to practice *at the chosen time*, (3) losing the momentum of a regular routine for practicing mindfulness, and (4) failing to successfully initiate mindfulness practice as a new behavior.

Ways to address this barrier include:

- "Piggyback" the mindfulness practice onto another already-established habit or behavior.
- Add visual reminders. Often these can be placed strategically directly in the line of vision, or in other places where they cannot be ignored or where they might physically block a client's progress as they go about their regular routine. These reminders may need to be changed after a period of time, if they lose the ability to capture the client's attention.
- Use timers when helpful. These can be either freestanding timers on existing devices such as cellphones or on appliances. Alternatively, they can be "natural" timers that occur in the environment, such as the end of a TV show, when 10:05 bus drives by, when the microwave beeps after reheating food, when the dog barks to come back inside, and so on.
- Add digital reminders (e.g., timers, alarms on electronic devices, electronic calendars).
- Apply other creative solutions developed by you and the client.

Case Example Using Object-Focused Mindfulness

A detailed case example is offered to demonstrate the level of detail that can be useful for many clients who present with this specific barrier, and also to illustrate a number of the suggestions discussed above. While some clients benefit from this detailed approach, others may need less.

After discussing his difficulties with practicing object-centered mindfulness using a polished stone, Ted felt that he had encountered several of the barriers mentioned earlier. He often remembered that he wanted to engage in mindfulness practice, but not at a time when he could complete it. Originally, he planned to engage in mindfulness practice throughout the day at work but found it difficult to remember at the designated time and to stop in the midst of his duties in order to practice. On a few occasions, he did remember at the designated time, but then did not complete the mindfulness practice. He had difficulty articulating what stopped him from practicing mindfulness, other than stating that "it just felt weird."

Knowing that Ted typically locks and unlocks several doors throughout the day, he and his therapist came up with the following new plan. His usual routine involves locking the house when he leaves for work, unlocking his car, driving to work, locking the car, and unlocking his office when he gets inside. This routine is reversed on the way home. He attached a polished stone key ring to his keys, and kept another in his left front pocket. In the new plan, when he leaves in the morning, he will lock the house, and see the stone on the key ring. Both will remind him it is almost time to engage in a mindfulness practice. He will then unlock the car, take the stone out of his pocket and hold it in his left hand. Then, he will get in and start the car, and focus on the stone for at least 3 minutes. Upon arrival at work, he will park his car, see the stone on the key ring, and again will be reminded that it is almost time to engage in a mindfulness practice. Once inside, he will unlock his office, take the stone out of his pocket and hold it in his left hand. Then he will sit down, and again focus on the stone for at least 3 minutes. When he is done, he will slip it back into his pocket. If he notices the stone in his pocket during the work day, and is able to take several minutes to focus on it, he will do so. If not, he will just notice it, take a breath, and know that later on, he will get back to it. Using the same routine described earlier, he will practice again when he gets into the car to go home, and also before leaving the car to enter the house. When he empties his pockets as he is getting undressed for the night, he will take a full 5 minutes to focus on the stone one last time for the day.

In this example, the mindfulness has been "piggybacked" onto the behavior of locking and unlocking doors. This behavior was chosen because it occurs at a time when he can take several minutes to be mindful, and in which pausing for this amount of time won't cause any problems. Ted liked the idea of letting the engine warm up for several minutes before driving, noting that it was better for the engine. The stone on the keychain acts as a visual reminder and as a transitional cue that "something new is coming" which helps with the "weird" feeling. Holding the stone in his hand prevents him from moving forward with his next usual behavior because he uses that hand to complete tasks such as reaching for his seat belt and typing his password at work. In the evening, the mindfulness practice is piggybacked onto the well-established habit of emptying his pockets. Though he felt that he could only give 3 minutes of time for the practice at the other times of day, he was agreeable to taking 5 minutes at the end of the day. When he was finished, the stone was placed back onto the dresser with his wallet, positioning it so that it was near his wallet, which helped him to remember to put the stone in his pocket.

2. Too Busy

Clients who identify being too busy as a barrier to practicing mindfulness may benefit from one or more of the following suggestions:

- Note that the Mindful Moments (informal) practice can be especially well-suited to a busy lifestyle.

- For dedicated (formal) mindfulness, collaborate with the client to identify times during the day when the client is already "doing" something else, but which involve periods of inactivity. Then match the type of mindfulness practice to what would work best in that setting. For example, if a client is quietly waiting with other people for a meeting to begin, focusing intently on one object may be noticeable and seem abnormal to others. However, in that same setting, a client could conduct a Body Scan, quietly focus on ambient sounds in the room or the breath, or observe with open awareness, noticing whatever crosses their field of awareness. Activities or tasks that include waiting can be very useful, including: an appointment, in line, children to arrive from school or to finish with an activity, and for other people. Other periods of inactivity may occur while riding on a bus, train, or subway, or during other daily activities.
- "Build" mindfulness practice into daily life, rather than trying to "fit it in." A practice time that is "built in" has a solid place in a person's daily routine. A specific period of time has been dedicated to the practice of mindfulness, with other activities falling in around it. "Fitting it in" gives the impression that the mindfulness practice will be done whenever some time happens to be available, which may not occur at all.
- Explore what "too busy" means to the client. If it's related to poor time management or poor time awareness, rather than a demanding set of obligations, then determine if any of the earlier-mentioned solutions (see Barrier #1) might be helpful.
- Examine the benefits and costs of practicing mindfulness, especially as it relates to the client's goals for treatment.
- Do the math. Help the client view the amount of Dedicated Mindfulness practice time in the context of their waking hours each day. If the goal is to practice Dedicated Mindfulness for 3–5 minutes, five times per day, that adds up to a total of 15–25 minutes spaced thought the day. If a person sleeps for 8 hours, that leaves 16 waking hours, which is 960 minutes. Converted into a percentage of waking hours, 15–25 minutes is equivalent to about 1.6%–2.6% of waking time each day. When seen in this context, the client may feel it is reasonable to make a commitment to engaging in the mindfulness practices.
- Sleep problems are very common among individuals with an AUD. Since "trying" to fall asleep usually has the opposite effect, why not engage in mindfulness practice instead? Practice at this time can be extended well beyond the minimum of 3–5 minutes. Even if sleep onset is delayed, the benefits of mindfulness can be obtained. In addition, practicing mindfulness at this time may have the added benefit of improving sleep.

3. Believes Practicing Mindfulness Won't Work for Them

Clients commonly cite certain personal traits or general beliefs about themselves that may prevent them from practicing mindfulness including the following:

- Difficulty concentrating, lack of focus, mind wanders, or easily side-tracked
- Feel uncomfortable sitting still or can't sit still for long periods of time. The client can view this as a personality trait (i.e., "always on the go"), a symptom from another diagnosis (hyperactivity, restlessness, anxiety) or a symptom of a chronic medical condition (e.g., back pain)
- Low self-efficacy (i.e., "I'm bad at that kind of thing")
- Too many thoughts (i.e., "I can't 'empty my mind'; it's impossible")

To address this particular barrier, explore the reasons the client can't practice mindfulness, and offer information relevant to their reasoning. Many of these reasons can be addressed by reinforcing rationale and information already provided in the session content and client workbook, and further elaborating on the attitudinal foundations of mindfulness. Other ways to address this belief include:

- Reviewing the steadily growing evidence for mindfulness-based treatment of depression, obsessive-compulsive disorder, and other conditions. While not a promise, it is possible that practicing mindfulness may also address some of the symptoms of other diagnoses.
- Start small: Some clients will benefit from starting with small and manageable practice goals. If the client is certain that they are "bad at this kind of thing," then mindfulness practice goals should be limited in order to demonstrate that they are capable.
- Highlighting times when the client is already being mindful without any effort. Most people will be able to describe times that they have been especially aware of the present moment. This may occur when listening to music, viewing an especially beautiful sunset, watching a TV show or movie that has them "on the edge of their seat," becoming engrossed in a book, holding a baby, being outdoors, singing a hymn in church, or eating a favorite food.
- Particularly when beginning mindfulness practice, people who have trouble sitting still can practice Dedicated Mindfulness while moving. If they need to shift position in the chair, then they may turn their attention to what it feels like to shift their body position. Walking is also a popular physical activity to use for mindfulness practice. As

the client progresses, they can decide to mindfully observe or watch for times when they no longer want to sit still.
- You may find that misconceptions about mindfulness may persist, even though the subject has already been discussed with the client. Be prepared to reinforce and elaborate on information that will help address the beliefs that "mindfulness" is not accessible or won't work for them. For example, if a client states that they are not good at concentrating, you can remind them that being able to focus is neither a requirement nor an expectation, although sometimes people do see improvements. Then review the material on how to respond to this barrier.

4. Doesn't Have Anything to Do With Drinking

Clients who have difficulty seeing the relevance of mindfulness as it relates to their problematic drinking may benefit from one or more of the following suggestions:

- Note that the specific skill of Urge Surfing, a specific type of mindfulness practice, has been used as an effective way to manage urges to drink for many years (Marlatt & Gordon, 1985).
- Review the information regarding the role of emotions in alcohol use and the use of mindfulness as an emotion regulation skill.
- Explain that the ability to stop yourself in the midst of a well-learned chain of behaviors, where each behavior leads to the next (habit), is at the core of making a successful behavior change. The regular practice of mindfulness can be very effective in learning to stop well-learned behaviors.
- Mindfulness is a way of directing one's attention such that the drinking cues or triggers lose some of their urgency or power to move the client toward drinking.

5. Easily Discouraged—"It didn't work"

- Examine the client's expectations and discuss the nonstriving attitudinal foundation that underlies mindfulness.
- Emphasize that time and practice will increase the benefit the client derives from mindfulness practices. It's important to stress the value of adopting the "nonstriving" mindset while continuing to engage in the mindfulness practices. The benefits will come simply by spending some time doing them that is, "The more you do it, the better you get."

6. Skeptical—"It won't work"

- Review the rationale for practicing mindfulness, describe mindfulness success stories from previous clients or personal experiences,

and convey enthusiasm and confidence regarding the effectiveness of mindfulness.
- Provide information about the other evidence-based treatments that utilize mindfulness for other problems or conditions (e.g., anxiety, PTSD, stress management, pain management, depression), choosing examples that may be most relevant for the client.

7. Goes Against Religious Practice or Spiritual Beliefs

- Although certain religions may promote meditation practices, the mindfulness practices described in the ERT are not part of any religion. Explore the client's specific concerns. For example, some people are suspicious of a mantra, believing it may be a way to summon malevolent spiritual entities. Share that many people find that mindfulness enhances their faith. For example, if a flower is chosen for an object-centered mindfulness exercise, the client can include the appreciation for the miracle of such a beautiful creation. If a client attends church, she may find that being in the present moment during the service can bring about a deep sense of spirituality and peace. During prayer, she can use the same technique of returning her attention to prayers when she finds her mind wandering.

8. Loses Motivation Over Time

- Identify other barriers to practice that may have developed for the client. Provide a review of the effectiveness and rationale of mindfulness. Consider reducing the amount of effort required by the client to engage in the practices. Many times, people can sustain a greater degree of effort at the beginning of a planned behavior change, but they are unable to sustain it over time. You may also review the client's goals for treatment and relate how the ongoing practice of mindfulness can contribute to reaching their goals.

9. Too Many Distractions

- When clients report they have no quiet time, become sleepy, or are interrupted by people or sounds, it's helpful to focus on adjusting their expectations and attitude toward distractions. Although it is nice to have a quiet space and time in which to engage in the Dedicated Mindfulness practices, it is not a requirement. Review the value of having a nonjudgmental attitude and how to continue practicing mindfulness by including the distractions into their mindful observations, breathing with and through any distractions. The clients can be encouraged to notice any negative thoughts or reactions, let them go, and return to the mindfulness practice.

Appendix B

Scene Development Worksheet

I'd like to ask about the times when you experience an unpleasant emotion and want to drink. *At the present time,* which situation involving unpleasant emotions would you say poses the greatest risk for drinking? (If the person has difficulty understanding the first question try another way: Currently, in what situation involving unpleasant emotions would you find it most difficult to abstain from drinking?)

Situation in person's own words: _____

Fill in details by asking the following questions:

1. Where are you? _____
2. Who else is with you? _____
3. What thoughts are going through your mind? _____

4. What are you feeling? (use the Emotions List, if necessary) _____

5. How strong is the emotion in this situation? _____
6. When you are feeling this emotion, where or how are you feeling it in your body? (e.g., heart pounding, upset stomach, shakiness, muscle tension) _____

7. At what point do you feel like drinking? _____

8. What would happen if you didn't have that drink? _____

9. How strong is your urge to drink in this situation? _____

Imagery Scene Description

Use the information gathered above and write three or four sentences that describe the negative emotional drinking situation.

Appendix C

Individual Distress Scale

In order to monitor changes in your level of emotion during the imagery scenes, we need to use a scale that is familiar to both of us. The individual distress scale below has numbers from 0 to 100 and indicates your level of discomfort. A rating of 100 indicates that you are extremely upset, the most you have ever been in your life, and a rating of 0 indicates no discomfort at all, or complete relaxation. Often when people say they have a rating of 100, they may be experiencing physical reactions such as sweaty palms, palpitations, difficulty breathing, feelings of dizziness, and anxiety. This scale is personalized to include examples of situations from your own life that elicit different levels of discomfort at each point on the scale.

Here is an example of one person's scale:
0 = watching TV in bed, very relaxed
25 = walking down the street during the day
50 = at home alone during the afternoon
75 = getting a phone call from my child's teacher
100 = like I felt when my partner left me

Identify personal situations for each of the 0, 25, 50, 75, and 100 scale points on this distress scale.

0 =

25 =

50 =

75 =

100 =

Appendix D

Direct Experiencing of Emotion Recording Form

Client _____ Date _____ Duration _____

Direct Experiencing of Emotion Scene _____

Time	Distress Rating	Craving Rating	Notes:
			Initial Ratings
			Post-Exposure Ratings

Appendix E

Relapse Prevention Plan

What skills, methods, and approaches have been most helpful or useful?

_____
_____
_____

What are my relapse warning signs? (from Session 11)

_____
_____
_____

What are some high-risk situations to keep in mind?

_____
_____
_____

Who can I reach out to for support? (List people, self-help groups, community organizations/groups, etc.)

_____
_____
_____

Any additional treatment needed at this time?

_____
_____
_____

References

Aldao, A., Nolen-Hoeksema, S., & Schweizer, S. (2010). Emotion regulation strategies across psychopathology: A meta-analytic review. *Clinical Psychology Review, 30,* 217–237.

Amsel, A. (1958). The role of frustrative nonreward in noncontinuous reward situations. *Psychological Bulletin, 55,* 102–119.

Annis, H. M., Turner, N. E., & Sklar, S. M. (1997). *Inventory of drug-taking situations: User's guide.* Toronto: Addiction Research Foundation of Ontario.

Back, S. E., Foa, E. B., Killeen, T. K., Mills, K. L., Teeson, M., Cotton, B., et al. (2015). *Concurrent treatment of PTSD and substance use disorders using prolonged exposure (COPE): Therapist guide.* New York, NY: Oxford University Press.

Baker, T. B., Morse, E., & Sherman, J. E. (1987). The motivation to use drugs: A psychobiological analysis of urges. In P. C. Rivers (Ed.), *The Nebraska symposium on motivation: Alcohol use and abuse* (pp. 257–323). Lincoln, NE: University of Nebraska Press.

Baker, T. B., Piper, M. E., McCarthy, D. E., Majeskie, M. R., & Fiore, M. C. (2004). Addiction motivation reformulated: An affective processing model of negative reinforcement. *Psychological Review, 111*(1), 33–51.

Bandura, A. (1986). *Social foundations of thought and action: A social cognitive theory.* Englewood Cliffs, NJ: Prentice-Hall.

Barlow, D. H., Allen, L. B., & Choate, M. L. (2004). Toward a unified treatment for emotional disorders. *Behavior Therapy, 35,* 205–230.

Barlow, D. H., Farchione, T. J., Fairholme, C. P., Ellard, K. K., Boisseau, C. L., Allen, L. B., et al. (2011). *Unified protocol for transdiagnostic treatment of emotional disorders.* New York, NY: Oxford University Press.

Berking, M., Margraf, M., Ebert, D., Wupperman, P., Hofmann, S. G., & Junghanns, K. (2011). Deficits in emotion-regulation skills predict alcohol use during and after cognitive-behavioral therapy for alcohol dependence. *Journal of Consulting and Clinical Psychology, 79*(3), 307–318.

Berking, M., & Whitley, B. (2014). *Affect regulation training: A practitioners' manual.* New York, NY: Springer.

Bien, T., & Bien, B. (2002). *Mindful recovery: A spiritual path to healing from addiction.* New York, NY: John Wiley & Sons.

Bowen, S., Chawla, N., & Marlatt, G. A. (2011). *Mindfulness-based relapse prevention for addictive behaviors: A clinician's guide.* New York, NY: Guilford Press.

Bradizza, C. M., Stasiewicz, P. R., & Paas, N. D. (2006). Relapse to alcohol and drug use among individuals diagnosed with co-occurring mental health and substance use disorders: A review. *Clinical Psychology Review: Special Issue: Relapse in the Addictive Behaviors, 2,* 162–178.

Bradizza, C. M., Stasiewicz, P. R., Zhuo, Y., Ruszczyk, M., Maisto, S. A., Brandon, T. H., et al. (2017). Smoking cessation for pregnant smokers: Development and pilot test of an Emotion Regulation Treatment (ERT) for negative affect smokers. *Nicotine and Tobacco Research, 19,* 578–584.

Brown, S. A., Irwin, M., & Schuckit, M. A. (1991). Changes in anxiety among abstinent male alcoholics. *Journal of Studies on Alcohol, 52,* 55–61.

Brown, S. A., & Schuckit, M. A. (1988). Changes in depression among abstinent alcoholics. *Journal of Studies on Alcohol, 49,* 412–417.

Carmody, T. P. (1989). Affect regulation, nicotine addiction, and smoking cessation. *Journal of Psychoactive Drugs, 21,* 331–342.

Cloitre, M., Koenen, K. C., Cohen, L. R., & Han, H. (2002). Skills training in affective and interpersonal regulation followed by exposure: A phase-based treatment for PTSD related to childhood abuse. *Journal of Consulting and Clinical Psychology, 70,* 1067–1074.

Coffey, S. F., Schumacher, J. A., Nosen, E., Littlefield, A. K., Henslee, A., Lappen, A., et al. (2016). Trauma-focused exposure therapy for chronic posttraumatic stress disorder in alcohol and drug dependent patients: A randomized clinical trial. *Psychology of Addictive Behaviors. Special Issue: Co-Occurring Posttraumatic Stress and Substance Use: Emerging Research on Correlates, Mechanisms, and Treatments, 30,* 778–790.

Coffey, S. F., Schumacher, J. A., Stasiewicz, P. R., Henslee, A. H., Baillie, L. E., & Landy, N. (2010). Craving and physiological reactivity to trauma and alcohol cues in posttraumatic stress disorder and alcohol dependence. *Experimental and Clinical Psychopharmacology, 18,* 340–349.

Conger, J. J. (1956). Alcoholism: Theory, problem and challenge. II. Reinforcement theory and the dynamics of alcoholism. *Quarterly Journal of Studies on Alcohol, 17*(2), 296–305.

Cooper, M. L., Frone, M. R., Russell, M., & Mudar, P. (1995). Drinking to regulate positive and negative emotions: A motivational model of alcohol use. *Journal of Personality and Social Psychology, 69*(5), 990–1005.

Cooper, M. L., Russell, M., Skinner, J. B., Frone, M. R., & Mudar, P. (1992). Stress and alcohol-use—moderating effects of gender, coping, and alcohol expectancies. *Journal of Abnormal Psychology, 101*(1), 139–152.

Desrosiers, A., Vine, V., Klemanski, D. H., & Nolen-Hoeksema, S. (2013). Mindfulness and emotion regulation in depression and anxiety: Common and distinct mechanisms of action. *Depression and Anxiety, 30*(7), 654–661.

Dvorak, R. D., Wray, T. B., Kuvaas, N. J., & Kilwein, T. M. (2013). Mania and sexual risk: Associations with behavioral self-regulation. *Journal of Affective Disorders, 150*(3), 1076–1081.

Farchione, T. J., Fairholme, C. P., Ellard, K. K., Boisseau, C. L., Thompson-Hollands, J., Carl, J. R., et al. (2012). Unified protocol for transdiagnostic treatment of emotional disorders: A randomized controlled trial. *Behavior Therapy, 43,* 666–678.

Foa, E. B., Hembree, E., & Rothbaum, B. O. (2007). *Prolonged exposure therapy for PTSD: Emotional processing of traumatic experiences.* New York, NY: Oxford University Press.

Fox, H. C., Hong, K. A., & Sinha, R. (2008). Difficulties in emotion regulation and impulse control in recently abstinent alcoholics compared with social drinkers. *Addictive Behaviors, 33*(2), 388–394.

Freud, S. (1936). *The problem of anxiety.* New York: Psychoanalytic Quarterly Press and W. W. Norton.

Goldfried, M. R. (1980). Toward the delineation of therapeutic change principles. *American Psychologist, 35,* 991–999.

Goldin, P. R., Lee, I., Ziv, M., Jazaieri, H., Heimberg, R. G., & Gross, J. J. (2014). Trajectories of change in emotion regulation and social anxiety during cognitive-behavioral therapy for social anxiety disorder. *Behaviour Research and Therapy, 56,* 7–15.

Gratz, K. L., Bardeen, J. R., Levy, R., Dixon-Gordon, K. L., & Tull, M. T. (2015). Mechanisms of change in an emotion regulation group therapy for deliberate self-harm among women with borderline personality disorder. *Behaviour Research and Therapy, 65,* 29–35.

Gratz, K. L., & Roemer, L. (2004). Multidimensional assessment of emotion regulation and dysregulation: Development, factor structure, and initial validation of the difficulties in emotion regulation scale. *Journal of Psychopathology and Behavioral Assessment, 26*(1), 41–54.

Gross, J. J. (1998). The emerging field of emotion regulation: An integrative review. *Review of General Psychology, 2,* 271–299.

Gross, J. J. (2013). Emotion regulation: Taking stock and moving forward. *Emotion, 13,* 359–365.

Gross, J. J. (2014). Emotion regulation: Conceptual and empirical foundations. In J. J. Gross (Ed.), *Handbook of emotion regulation* (2nd ed.). New York, NY: The Guilford Press.

Gross, J. J., & John, O. P. (2003). Individual differences in two emotion regulation processes: Implications for affect, relationships, and well-being. *Journal of Personality and Social Psychology, 85*(2), 348–362.

Hayes, A. M., & Feldman, G. (2004). Clarifying the construct of mindfulness in the context of emotion regulation and the process of change in therapy. *Clinical Psychology-Science and Practice, 11*(3), 255–262.

Hayes, A. M., Feldman, G., Beevers, C., Laurenceau, J. P., Cardaciotto, L., & Lewis-Smith, J. (2007). Discontinuities and cognitive changes in exposure-based cognitive therapy for depression. *Journal of Consulting and Clinical Psychology, 75,* 409–421.

Holahan, C. J., Moos, R. H., Holahan, C. K., Cronkite, R. C., & Randall, P. K. (2001). Drinking to cope, emotional distress and alcohol use and abuse: A ten-year model. *Journal of Studies on Alcohol, 62*(2), 190–198.

Holahan, C. J., Moos, R. H., Holahan, C. K., Cronkite, R. C., & Randall, P. K. (2003). Drinking to cope and alcohol use and abuse in unipolar depression: A 10-year model. *Journal of Abnormal Psychology, 112*(1), 159–165.

Hunt, W. A., Barnett, L. W., & Branch, L. G. (1971). Relapse rates in addiction programs. *Journal of Clinical Psychiatry, 27,* 455–456.

Kabat-Zinn, J. (1990). *Full catastrophe living: Using the wisdom of your body and mind to face, stress, pain, and illness.* New York, NY: Delacorte.

Kadden, R. M., Carroll, K. M., Donovon, D., Cooney, N., Monti, P., Abrams, D. B., et al. (1992). *Cognitive-behavioral coping skills therapy manual: A clinical research guide for therapists treating individuals with alcohol abuse and dependence.* NIAAA Project Match Monograph (D. P. N. A. 92–1895, ed., Vol. 3). Washington, DC: Government Printing Office.

Kazdin, A. E. (2007). Mediators and mechanisms of change in psychotherapy research. *Annual Review of Clinical Psychology, 3,* 1–27.

Khantzian, E. J. (1997). The self-medication hypothesis of substance use disorders: A reconsideration and recent applications. *Harvard Review of Psychiatry, 4*(5), 231–244.

Koob, G. F. (2003). Alcoholism: Allostasis and beyond. *Alcoholism: Clinical & Experimental Research, 27,* 232–243.

Koob, G. F., & LeMoal, M. (2001). Drug addiction, dysregulation of reward, and allostasis. *Neuropsychopharmacology, 24,* 97–129.

Koob, G. F., & Volkow, N. D. (2010). Neurocircuitry of addiction. *Neuropsychopharmacology, 35,* 217–238.

Linehan, M. M. (1993). *Skills training manual for treating borderline personality disorder.* New York, NY: Guilford Press.

Linehan, M. M. (2015). *DBT skills training manual* (2nd ed.). New York, NY: Guilford Press.

Lowman, C., Allen, J., Stout, R. L., & The Relapse Research Group. (1996). Replication and extension of Marlatt's taxonomy or relapse precipitants: Overview of procedures and results. *Addiction, 91*(Suppl.), S51–S71.

Maisto, S. A., Carey, K. B., & Bradizza, C. M. (1999). Social learning theory. In K. E. Leonard & H. T. Blane (Eds.), *Psychological theories of drinking and alcoholism* (2nd ed., pp. 106–163). New York, NY: Guilford Press.

Marlatt, G. A., & Gordon, J. R. (Eds.). (1985). *Relapse prevention: Maintenance strategies in the treatment of addictive behaviors.* New York, NY: Guilford Press.

Mennin, D. S., & Fresco, D. M. (2014). Emotion regulation therapy. In J. J. Gross (Ed.), *Handbook of emotion regulation* (2nd ed., pp. 469–490). New York, NY: The Guilford Press.

Neacsiu, A. D., Eberle, J. W., Kramer, R., Wiesmann, T., & Linehan, M. M. (2014). Dialectical behavior therapy skills for transdiagnostic emotion dysregulation: A pilot randomized controlled trial. *Behaviour Research and Therapy, 59,* 40–51.

O'Brien, C. P., Ehrman, R. N., & Ternes, J. W. (1986). Classical conditioning in human opioid dependence. In S. R. Goldberg & I. P. Stolerman (Eds.), *Behavioral analysis of drug dependence.* Orlando, FL: Academic Press.

Oliver, J. A., MacQueen, D. A., & Drobes, D. J. (2013). Deprivation, craving, and affect: Intersecting constructs in addiction. In P. M. Miller (Ed.), *Comprehensive addictive behaviors and disorders, Vol 1: Principles of addiction* (pp. 395–403). Saint Louis, MO: Academic Press.

Phan, K. L., Wager, T., Taylor, S. F., & Liberzon, I. (2002). Functional neuroanatomy of emotion: A meta-analysis of emotion activation studies in PET and fMRI. *Neuroimage, 16,* 331–348.

Sayers, W. M., & Sayette, M. A. (2013). Suppression on your own terms: Internally generated displays of craving suppression predict rebound effects. *Psychological Science, 24,* 1740–1746.

Segal, Z. V., Williams, J. M. G., & Teasdale, J. D. (2002). *Mindfulness-based cognitive therapy for depression: A new approach to preventing relapse.* New York, NY: The Guilford Press.

Seo, D., & Sinha, R. (2014). The neurobiology of alcohol craving and relapse. In E. V. Sullivan & A. Pfefferbaum (Eds.), *Handbook of clinical neurology: Alcohol and the nervous system* (Vol. 125, pp. 355–368). Waltham, MA: Elsevier.

Sinha, R., Fox, H. C., Hong, K., A., Berquist, K., Bhagwagar, Z., & Siedlarz, K. M. (2009). Enhanced negative emotion and alcohol craving, and altered physiological responses following stress and cue exposure in alcohol dependent individuals. *Neuropsychopharmacology, 34,* 1198–1208.

Sobell, L. C., Toneatto, T., & Sobell, M. B. (1994). Behavioral-assessment and treatment planning for alcohol, tobacco, and other drug problems—current status with an emphasis on clinical-applications. *Behavior Therapy, 25*(4), 533–580.

Stampfl, T. G. (1991). Analysis of aversive events in human psychopathology: Fear and avoidance. In M. R. Denny (Ed.), *Fear, avoidance, and phobias: A fundamental analysis.* Hillsdale, NJ: Lawrence Erlbaum Associates.

Stasiewicz, P. R., Bradizza, C. M., Gudleski, G. D., Coffey, S. F., Schlauch, R. C., Bailey, S. T., et al. (2012). The relationship of alexithymia to emotional dysregulation within an alcohol dependent treatment sample. *Addictive Behaviors, 37,* 469–476.

Stasiewicz, P. R., Bradizza, C. M., Schlauch, R. C., Coffey, S. F., Gulliver, S. B., Gudleski, G., et al. (2013). Affect regulation training (ART) for alcohol dependence: Development of a novel intervention for negative affect drinkers. *Journal of Substance Abuse Treatment, 45,* 433–443.

Stasiewicz, P. R., Bradizza, C. M., & Slosman, K. S. (2014). Affect regulation training for alcohol use disorders: Learning to engage with negative emotions. *Counselor, 15,* 64–71.

Stasiewicz, P. R., & Maisto, S. A. (1993). Two-factor avoidance theory: The role of negative affect in the maintenance of substance use and substance use disorder. *Behavior Therapy, 24,* 337–356.

Tiffany, S. T. (1990). A cognitive model of drug urges and drug-use behavior: Role of automatic and nonautomatic processes. *Psychological Review, 97,* 147–168.

Tiffany, S. T. (2010). Drug craving and affect. In J. D. Kassel (Ed.), *Substance abuse and emotion* (pp. 83–108). Washington, DC: American Psychological Association.

Treanor, M. (2011). The potential impact of mindfulness on exposure and extinction learning in anxiety disorders. *Clinical Psychology Review, 31*(4), 617–625.

Tschacher, W., Junghan, U. M., & Pfammatter, M. (2014). Towards a taxonomy of common factors in psychotherapy—results of an expert survey. *Clinical Psychology and Psychotherapy, 21,* 82–96.

Index

Note: Page numbers in **bold** refer to tables.

abstinence-based treatment 24–25
Adaptive Coping with Emotions **16**
affective experiencing 17
affect regulation: defined 2; interventions targeting **16**
Affect Regulation Training **16**
Affect Regulation Treatment (ART) *see* Emotion Regulation Treatment (ERT) program
Alcoholics Anonymous (AA) 133, 134
alcohol use disorder (AUD): co-occurring disorders with 18; craving and 20–22; emotion regulation skills and 3–5; emotions role in 1–2; identifying emotion regulation difficulties in 5–7; social support and 130–131
Allen, L. B. **16**
American Psychologist 14
Amsel, A. 21
antecedent-focused strategies 3
anxiety disorders, AUD treatment and 18
AUD *see* alcohol use disorder (AUD)
awareness activities 34

Barlow, D. H. **16**
behavior therapy, "third wave" of 14
Berking, M. **16**
between-session skill practice *see* skill practice
body scan 48–50, 53–54
Bowen, S. **16**
Bradizza, C. M. **16**
breathalyzer test 41, 53, 64, 77, 92, 104, 112, 129, 144, 155, 164, 172

CBT Triangle model 43, 97–99
Choate, M. L. **16**
client rapport and engagement 41–42
client workbook *see* Managing Negative Emotions Without Drinking (client workbook)
Cloitre, M. **16**
Coffey, S. F. **16**
cognitive avoidance 33
cognitive-behavioral therapy (CBT) 4, 7–8, 19, 43
Cognitive Reappraisal: as antecedent-focused 83; defined 83–84; examples of 85, 87–88; in-session skill practice 89–90; managing emotions with 3, 5, 46, 82–90; skills, implementing 86–87; thought to emotion and behavior relationship 84
coping 2
corrective emotional experience 17
craving: as conditioned response (CR) 20; emotion and 20–22; negative emotions and 20–21; positive emotions and 21; substance-related cues, exposure to 21–22

Daily Monitoring Log: Cognitive Reappraisals and 89; described 12–13; drinking-related thoughts/coping skills 79; drink refusal skills and 93; for high-risk situations 65; lapse/relapse and 112–113, 121, 127; for motivation/mindfulness 56; Naming the Emotion and 76; for progress review 155–156, 162; for relapse prevention 164–165,

170; review of, with client 50–51; seemingly irrelevant decisions and 144–145, 153; for successful skill use/progress 172; support network building and 129–130, 137, 142; treatment goal progress and 104–105
Daily Relapse Prevention worksheet 166
decisional balance for abstinence exercise 57
Dedicated Mindfulness 50, 75–76
detoxification program 25
Dialectical Behavior Therapy **16**, 17
Difficulties in Emotion Regulation Scale (DERS) 5–6
direct experiencing of emotion recording form 111, 120, 123, 126, 128, 137, 139–140, 143, 149–150, 154, 160, 187
direct experiencing of emotions 5, 14–16, **16**; pause and hold technique 136–137; preparing for 107–108; processing of 126–127, 152; rating scales 120–121; rationale, engaging with negative emotions 118–120, 135; recording form 187; review of previous 147–150; session 2 of 4 135–142; session 3 of 4 147–153; session 4 of 4 158–162; strategy for managing 45–46; therapy techniques 17–18; using imaginal exposure 121–126, 137–142
direct social pressure 93–94
distress tolerance 2
drinking-related thoughts: coping skills 80–82; noticing 80
drink refusal skills 93–97; examples of 95; rationale for 93–95; role play 95–96; social pressures and 93–94

Ehrman, R. N. 21–22
emotional awareness, increasing 48
emotion-craving-drinking connection, direct experiencing of emotion and 35–36
emotion regulation 68–73; assessment of 5–6; avoidance/suppression of negative emotions 68–71; emotion-craving wave and 68; Daily Monitoring Log review 65; defined 2, 3; informal mindfulness practices 74–75; intervention, goals of 3; skills, AUD and 3–5; strategies, of ERT program 8; successful skill use/ progress, reinforce 64–65; therapy techniques 17–18; Watch the Wave skills 63, 71
Emotion Regulation Questionnaire (ERQ) 5, 6
Emotion Regulation Therapy **16**
Emotion Regulation Treatment (ERT) program **16**; as abstinence-based treatment 24–25; administering, persons qualified for 9; client workbook, use of 13; components of 12; co-occurring disorders and 18; craving and 20–22; development of 7–9; direct experiencing of negative emotion and 32–34; direct experiencing of unpleasant emotions 14–16, **16**; emotion regulation strategies of 8; emotions, discussing role of 31–32; higher level of care referrals 25; identifying AUD 5–7; imaginal exposure, direct experiencing of emotion via 34–38; introducing client to 23–25; introduction to 1–13; exposure to a negative emotional drinking situation *vs.* exposure to traumatic events 18–19; outline of 9–12; rationale for 1–5; Session 1 40–52; Session 2 53–62; Session 3 63–76; Session 4 77–91; Session 5 92–102; Session 6 103–110; Session 7 111–127; Session 8 128–142; Session 9 143–153; Session 10 154–162; Session 11 163–170; Session 12 171–176; session structure 12–13; skill practice, in-session/ between session 25–30; theory/ research supporting 3–4; therapist-client relationship, collaborative 30–31; therapy techniques 17–18; traumatic event disclosure during 19–20; treatment strategies 5; *see also individual sessions*
emotions: cognitive reappraisal strategy for managing 46, 82–90; craving and 20–22; daily life, discuss with client 31; direct experiencing of 5; direct experiencing of, using mindfulness

and imaginal exposure therapeutic techniques 32–34; drinking and 68–69; managing, with direct experiencing strategy 45–46; mindfulness strategy for managing 45; naming 75, 76; negative and positive, drinking and 6–7; preparing for direct experiencing of 107–108; primary 7; in problem drinking/relapse to drinking, role of 31–32; role of, in AUD 1–2; secondary, importance of 7; taking action strategy for managing 45; unpleasant, direct experiencing of 14–16, 16
emotions, managing with actions 97–102; between-session skill practice 102; CBT Triangle model 97–98; in-session skill practice 100; rationale 97–100; steps in process of 100–101; urge to act and 99–100
emotion Scene Development, direct experiencing of 109–110
Enhancing Social Support Networks 134
ERT *see* Emotion Regulation Treatment (ERT) program
Exposure-Based Cognitive Therapy 16
exposure sessions 10

Foa, E. 16, 18
Fresco, D. M. 16
Freud, S. 14
frustration 21

Gautama, S. 14
Goldfried, M. R. 14
Gross, J. J. 3; process model of emotion 3
guided imagery lemon exercise 108–109

Hayes, A. M. 16
Health and Lifestyles (HLS) control condition 8
Hembree, E. 16
high-risk situations 65–71; categories of common 67–68; defined 65–66; difficulty identifying 66–67; exploring client's 66; identifying 65
hit pause 59

imaginal exposure, direct experiencing of emotion via 34–38, 137–142; conducting 138–140; emotion-craving-drinking connection and 35–36; instructional set for 137–138; over-engagement in 37–38; post-exposure processing 140–142; rationale for 34–35; second presentation of 142; under-engagement in 36–37
indirect social pressure 94
Individual Distress Scale 111, 120–121, 128, 186
Inventory of Drug Taking Situations-Alcohol (IDTS-A) 6

Kazdin, A. E. 18
keep our batteries charged skill 169–170

labeling emotions skills 63
lapse: defined 117; strategies to use following 117–118
lifestyle balance 166–170
Lifestyle Balance Action Plan 170
Linehan, M. M. 16

Managing Negative Emotions Without Drinking (client workbook) 1; Session 1 use 40; Session 2 use 53, 56, 57; Session 3 use 63, 66, 73–74; Session 4 use 77, 80, 89, 90; Session 5 use 92, 100; Session 6 use 103, 110; Session 7 use 111, 117–118; Session 8 use 128, 134; Session 9 use 143; Session 10 use 154, 158; Session 11 use 163, 165, 166; Session 12 use 171, 175; use of 13
Mennin, D. S. 16
Menu of Coping Skills and Strategies 165
Mindful Breathing skills 63, 71–74
Mindful Moments 63, 74–75; 76
mindfulness 5, 10, 11, 18; barriers to practice of 177–183; definition of 75; direct experiencing of emotion using 32–34; informal 74–75; managing emotions via 45; object-focused 34, 60–62, 64, 178–179; understanding 58–59

Index

Mindfulness-Based Relapse
    Prevention **16**
Mindful Observing 59–60
mood disorders, AUD treatment
    and 18

Narcotics Anonymous (NA) 134
National Institute on Alcohol Abuse
    and Alcoholism (NIAAA) 10
negative affect drinking,
    measurement of 6
negative emotions: craving responses
    and 20–21; drinking and 6–7;
    vs. traumatic event 18–19; as
    unpleasant 47

Object-Centered Mindfulness 34,
    60–62, 64
O'Brien, C. P. 21–22
Opposite Action 17
outcome expectancies 1
over-engagement 37–38

pause and hold technique 128,
    136–137
positive emotions: craving and 21;
    drinking and 6–7; as pleasant 47
primary emotions 7
Project MATCH 10
Prolonged Exposure (modified) **16**
Prolonged Exposure
    Therapy **16**, 17

Rational Recovery 134
rebound effects 69
referrals to higher level of care 25
relapse, defined 117
relapse, preventing/coping with
    113–117; introduction to 113–114;
    major life events and 114–117
relapse prevention 165–166
relapse prevention plan 116, 165,
    171, 175–176, 188
relapse warning signs: information
    sheet 165
response-focused strategies 3
Rothbaum, B. O. **16**

Scene Development worksheet 103,
    109, 128, 143, 154, 161, 184–185
secondary emotions, importance of 7

seemingly irrelevant decisions (SIDs)
    145–147
self-efficacy expectations 1
self-help support groups 133–134
self-monitoring record, reviewing 13
Session 1, ERT program 40–52;
    between-session skill practice
    51–52; body scan 48–50;
    breathalyzer test 41; Daily
    Monitoring Log 50–51; Dedicated
    Mindfulness 50; emotional
    awareness, increasing 48;
    emotions, described 47–48;
    emotions and alcohol 43–45;
    general treatment overview 42–43;
    introduction 41–42; managing
    emotions 45–46; materials 40;
    outline 40; overview 40; Stop and
    Notice skill 50
Session 2, ERT program 53–62;
    between-session skill practice 62;
    decisional balance for abstinence
    exercise 57–58; in-session
    skill practice 57–58, 60–62;
    introduction 53–57; making
    it happen 62; materials 53;
    mindfulness understanding 58–59;
    Mindful Observing 59–60; object-
    centered mindfulness 60–62; outline
    53; overview 53
Session 3, ERT program 63–76;
    between-session skill practice
    75–76; emotion regulation 68–73;
    high-risk situations 65–71;
    introduction 64; materials 63;
    Mindful Breathing 71–73; outline
    63; overview 63
Session 4, ERT program 77–91;
    between-session skill practice
    90–91; cognitive reappraisal to
    manage emotions 82–90; drinking-
    related thoughts and coping skills
    79–82; in-session skill practice
    89–90; introduction 77–79;
    materials 77; negative emotion
    drinking situation, applying skills to
    89–90; outline 77; overview 77
Session 5, ERT program 92–102;
    between-session skill practice
    102; drink refusal skills 93–97;
    emotions, managing with actions

97–102; introduction 92–93; materials 92; outline 92; overview 92
Session 6, ERT program 103–110; between-session skill practice 110; direct experiencing of emotion, preparing for 107–108; guided imagery lemon exercise 108–109; introduction 104–105; materials 103; outline 104; overview 103; Scene Development, direct experiencing of emotion 109–110; skills review 106–107; treatment progress/goals review 105–106
Session 7, ERT program 111–127; between-session skill practice 127; direct experiencing of emotion, introduction to 118–127; goals 111; introduction 112–113; lapse/relapse, getting back to abstinent after 117–118; materials 111; outline 111; relapse, preventing/coping with 113–117
Session 8, ERT program 128–142; between-session skill practice 142; direct experiencing of emotion 135–142; in-session skill practice 134; introduction 129–130; materials 128; outline 128; overview 128; social support networks 130–134
Session 9, ERT program 143–153; between-session skill practice 153; direct experiencing of emotion 147–153; in-session exercise 147; introduction 144–145; materials 143; outline 143; overview 143; seemingly irrelevant decisions (SIDs) 145–147; "The Story of SID" 145–146
Session 10, ERT program 154–162; between-session skill practice 162; direct experiencing of emotion, final session 158–162; introduction 155–156; materials 154; outline 154; overview 154; progress towards treatment goals 156; stimulus control 156–158
Session 11, ERT program 163–170; between-session skill practice 170; in-session skill practice 169–170;

introduction 164–165; lifestyle balance 166–170; materials 163; outline 163; overview 163; relapse prevention 165–166
Session 12, ERT program 171–176; alcohol-related thoughts, return of 174; introduction 172; materials 171; outline 172; overview 171; progress reinforcement 174; progress review 173; Relapse Prevention Plan review 175–176; skills review 173
SIDs (seemingly irrelevant decisions) 145–147
skill practice 25–30; acquisition of, facilitating 25–26; barriers to, problem solving 28–30; between-session, categories of 26–27; between-session, therapist support of 26; completing between-session, motivation for 27–28; negotiation 27; review 27; Session 1 51–52; Session 2 62; Session 3 73–74, 75–76; Session 4 89–90, 90–91; set-up 27
Skills Training in Affect and Interpersonal Regulation 16
slip, defined 117
SMART Recovery 134
social learning theory, alcohol use and 1
social support networks 130–134; AUD and 130–131; building 131–133; expansion of 133; in-session skill practice 134; overview of 130; self-help groups as 133–134; skill guidelines 131
SOS 134
Stasiewicz, P. R. 16
stimulus control 156–158
Stop and Notice skill 34, 50, 51, 59–60, 100
substance-related cues, negative affect following exposure to 21–22
suppression, defined 33

taking action strategy for managing emotions 45

Ternes, J. W. 21–22
Therapist Direct Experiencing of Emotion Recording Form 160
therapists: background/qualifications 41; client relationship, collaborative 30–31; qualified to administer ERT 9
"Toward the Delineation of Therapeutic Change Principles" (Goldfried) 14
traumatic event: disclosure during treatment, managing 19–20; *vs.* negative emotional drinking 18–19

under-engagement 36–37
Unified Protocol for the Treatment of Emotional Disorders **16**
unpleasant emotional response, time course of 68
urge surfing 17–18, 71

Watch the Wave skills 63, 71, 72, 76
weekly skill practice assignments, reviewing 13
white bear test 69

Helping you to choose the right eBooks for your Library

Add Routledge titles to your library's digital collection today. Taylor and Francis ebooks contains over 50,000 titles in the Humanities, Social Sciences, Behavioural Sciences, Built Environment and Law.

Choose from a range of subject packages or create your own!

Benefits for you
- Free MARC records
- COUNTER-compliant usage statistics
- Flexible purchase and pricing options
- All titles DRM-free.

Benefits for your user
- Off-site, anytime access via Athens or referring URL
- Print or copy pages or chapters
- Full content search
- Bookmark, highlight and annotate text
- Access to thousands of pages of quality research at the click of a button.

REQUEST YOUR FREE INSTITUTIONAL TRIAL TODAY

Free Trials Available
We offer free trials to qualifying academic, corporate and government customers.

eCollections – Choose from over 30 subject eCollections, including:

Archaeology	Language Learning
Architecture	Law
Asian Studies	Literature
Business & Management	Media & Communication
Classical Studies	Middle East Studies
Construction	Music
Creative & Media Arts	Philosophy
Criminology & Criminal Justice	Planning
Economics	Politics
Education	Psychology & Mental Health
Energy	Religion
Engineering	Security
English Language & Linguistics	Social Work
Environment & Sustainability	Sociology
Geography	Sport
Health Studies	Theatre & Performance
History	Tourism, Hospitality & Events

For more information, pricing enquiries or to order a free trial, please contact your local sales team: www.tandfebooks.com/page/sales

 Routledge
Taylor & Francis Group

The home of Routledge books

www.tandfebooks.com